Effective Supervisory Practices

BETTER RESULTS THROUGH TEAMWORK

D0117389

SECOND EDITION

Published for
The ICMA Training Institute
by the
International City
Management Association

Published in cooperation with
The Carl Vinson
Institute of Government,
University of Georgia

ICMA, the professional association
of appointed administrators
serving cities, counties, regional councils,
and other local governments

Library of Congress Cataloging in Publication Data
Main entry under title:

Effective supervisory practices.

  (Municipal management series)
  Bibliography: p.
  Includes index.
  1. Local government—Personnel management.   2. Local officials and employees.   3. Supervision of employees.
I. ICMA Training Institute.   II. International City Management Association.   III. Series.
JS155.E47   1984   352'.0051   84-10950
ISBN 0-87326-042-2

9089

Effective Supervisory Practices

BETTER RESULTS THROUGH TEAMWORK

SECOND EDITION

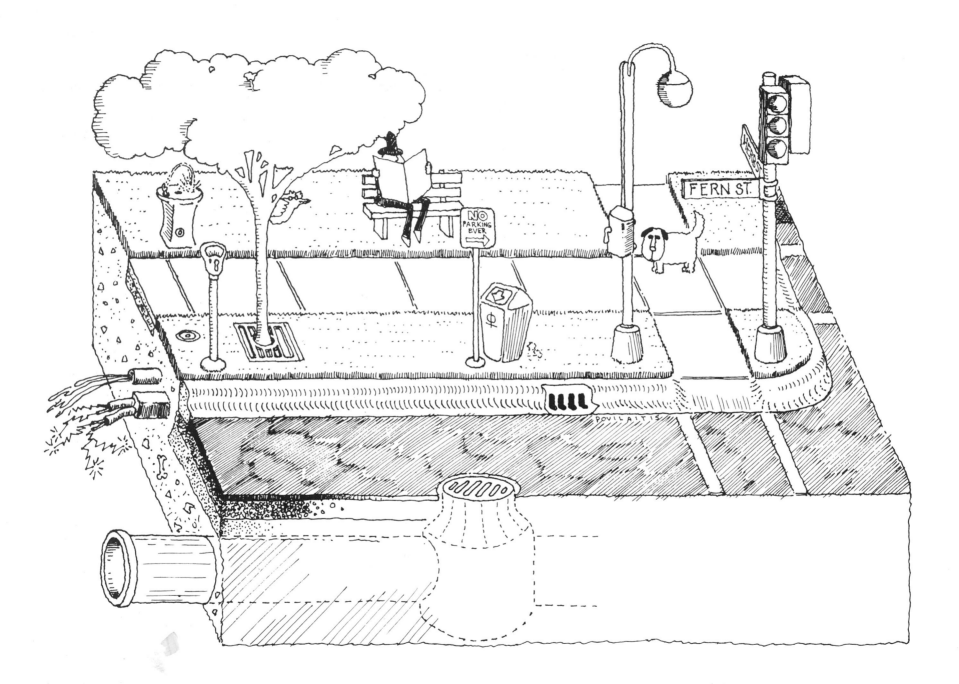

Where this book is going

This book has been written for experienced supervisors who want to become more effective managers, as well as for those who have been recently appointed to supervisory positions in local government.

Local governments exist for many purposes, but the overriding one is to provide public services. These services may be as specific as the police officer on preventive patrol or the street maintenance crew patching a road, or as intangible as a social service aide advising a middle-aged woman about potential employment. But all of these services are real, and you are involved in them because this is the public's work.

Good local government does not just happen. It happens because an informed citizenry, elected officials, conscientious public managers, and dedicated employees work together to make it happen. You can take pride in being a part of this effort to provide such vital traditional services as police, fire, tax assessment, sanitation, water supply, and street construction and maintenance, as well as many new services such as programs for the elderly, consumer education, housing relocation, and special education. These services are provided through local government organizations: city and county departments, divisions, offices, units, shifts, stations, and crews that keep government operating twenty-four hours a day.

When we talk about the public's work, it means that your work is done in the context of a public organization. This means that the public—through elected officials, boards and commissions, and many types of governmental processes—helps determine what your organization will do. Often, this public organization concept is what actually sets your goals and priorities.

Effective Supervisory Practices takes this larger framework of your local government and brings it within the scope of your job and the way you work with your employees. The emphasis on goals, on looking ahead, encourages you to consider where you are going rather than where you have been. Certainly, we all need to look back to learn from our mistakes, but much of this book addresses planning, leadership, motivation, and other aspects of working with people, so that you, as a supervisor, can do a better job of getting work done with and through others.

This book serves as the basic text for a training program designed to help you and your local government provide better services to people. The book and correlative training materials bring together basic principles of supervision, up-to-date findings from behavioral studies and other appropriate research, and practical, how-to-do-it guidelines for improving your supervisory skills and applying effective supervisory practices on the job.

The training approach

Though much of the material in this book is presented as simple models or step-by-step guidelines, or in the form of checklists, effective supervision is much more than models, guidelines, and checklists. It is a dynamic process—in part an art. But the art of supervision must be practiced on a solid foundation of knowledge with mastery of a wide variety of skills. This art of supervision also requires that you have the ability to adapt to the ever changing requirements of modern management.

This book is intended to help you by serving as a blueprint for fashioning a personal approach to supervision—an approach that will fit your personality, background, and work experiences, the unique nature of your supervisory position, and the special requirements of the local government organization you serve. It will help you bring together the processes of the job and the people who do the work so that services can be delivered more effectively to the citizens in your community.

A standard format is used in this book to facilitate reading, note taking, and group discussion. Each chapter leads off with a few questions to set the pace and guide later discussion. Primary and secondary heads are used to organize the text, and each chapter includes a checklist to summarize major points in the text. Illustrations and captions are also used to highlight major points in the text.

We hope that many supervisors will find a number of chapters sufficiently stimulating to make them want to explore these subjects further. We have, therefore, provided a brief bibliography at the end of the book.

By balancing group discussions and your own efforts in using the book, you can improve your supervisory skills.

International City Management Association

Training programs are provided by hundreds of organizations in the United States and Canada, including the continuing education provided by university extension agencies, the correspondence and on-site short courses sponsored by professional and trade associations, and the almost countless offerings of the commercial and nonprofit schools.

The International City Management Association (ICMA), since its founding in 1914, has set its sights on two major objectives: improving the professional competence of local government chief administrators and improving the management of local government in general.

Since 1934, the Institute for Training in Municipal Administration, sponsored by ICMA, has provided correspondence courses for on-the-job training of local government managers and supervisors. Many of the courses are based on ICMA's Municipal Management Series. In 1978, the ITMA was redesignated the ICMA Training Institute with a broader, two-fold mission: (1) to strengthen the capacity of local governments to develop their own, self-run training programs, and (2) to provide directly a much wider range of courses, training materials, and services for local government training and employee development.

In 1965 the first version of this book, prepared by Robert E. Bouton, was published as a series of fifteen bulletins in a three-ring binder. In 1978 a completely revised version of *Effective Supervisory Practices* was prepared by the University of Georgia's Institute of Government and Center for Continuing Education. This book, the second edition, has been prepared by the same organization, now designated the Governmental Training Division of the University of Georgia's Carl Vinson Institute of Government and Georgia Center for Continuing Education.

Those who worked on this book

All who have contributed to the writing of *Effective Supervisory Practices* are broadly experienced in local government. They have had many years of management or consulting experience in a variety of local governments across the country, ranging from large cities to small rural counties. They have emphasized the practical dimensions—the practices that work and the skills that are necessary for effective supervision.

Primary responsibility for this work was undertaken by Harold F. Holtz, Administrator of the Governmental Training Division. Others in the University's Governmental Training Division who revised or wrote selected chapters were: John F. Azzaretto, Assistant Administrator; Kitty Williams Clarke, Management Development Consultant; Kenneth K. Henning, Director of the Certified Manager Program; Janine P. Mills, Management Development Associate; and Howard N. Smith, Jr., Management Development Associate.

We are grateful to four persons who thoroughly reviewed all of the chapter drafts and provided helpful comments for final preparation of the manuscript: Walter Barry, City Administrator, North Kansas City, Missouri; Christine S. Becker, Director of Education Services, International City Management Association; Clifford R. Vermilya, Town Manager, Bloomfield, Connecticut; and Mac White, Personnel Director, Plano, Texas.

The Municipal Management Series is the responsibility of Barbara H. Moore, Senior Editor, ICMA. Other ICMA staff members who worked on this book were David S. Arnold, who had primary editorial responsibility and worked closely with the University's Governmental Training Division faculty and staff in planning and developing the text and illustrations; Christine S. Becker, who was active in the early planning of the book and reviewed all of the manuscript; and Christine Ulrich, who handled final editing and assisted in the final checking of manuscript and illustrations.

Herbert Slobin handled graphic design and layout. Illustrations were prepared by David Povilaitis and Herbert Slobin.

The International City Management Association is grateful to the faculty and staff of the Carl Vinson Institute of Government and Georgia Center for Continuing Education, University of Georgia, for the development of this book. In addition, and speaking in a more personal way, we are grateful to each of these persons for their enthusiasm for this project, for the many hours they have devoted to it, and for the great interest they have shown in making management a more effective part of local government.

William H. Hansell, Jr.
Executive Director

International City
Management Association

supervisor

/sü-pər-ˌvī-zər/ *noun* **1:** a member of the management team, *esp.* foremen and others in management jobs, in charge of persons directly carrying out work **2:** a person in a management job forming a direct link between management and workers **3:** a person responsible for getting work done through others **4:** a person who plans, organizes, directs, and evaluates work **5:** a person who applies problem solving and communication skills to jobs, tasks, activities, and management and employee relations **6:** a representative of management who introduces and facilitates change in the working environment **7:** a representative of management and the workers responsible for getting results through teamwork.

clear that you *are* saying "no." Do not use evasive or ambiguous words that might lead the person to think that you have said "maybe." If it is possible to refer the person somewhere else for more information or help, by all means do so, and avoid at all costs the attitude and demeanor of a judge pronouncing sentence on a culprit.

The media

The news media—newspapers, radio, and television—consider governmental news coverage one of their most important jobs. Since most people are intensely interested in local government developments, it is helpful for you to be familiar with what news means and how the media work.

News is the reporting of an event by words, sound, or pictures, with timely information for the general public. News is gathered, evaluated, and written up by trained reporters who often have a particular interest in major decisions that affect individual lives—increases or decreases in property taxes, approvals or disapprovals for the location of shopping centers, adoption of bond issues, and location of streets and highways. Newspapers (more than radio and television) often are interested in reporting not only the event but some of the circumstances behind the event. For example, a newspaper account may describe an urban renewal or urban redevelopment project and also provide information on the federal grants, programs, and conditions that made the project possible.

News reporters are likely to talk first to the mayor, the city or county manager, members of the city council or county board, and department heads. They know that these are the sources for the most complete information on events, particularly policy and management decisions. If your city or county has a public information officer, news reporters will turn to that person to get information. The public information officer generally has experience that helps him or her spot the news taking place and can provide fast and competent help for reporters. It is his or her job to establish good working relations with media representatives. A background in journalism can help.

If a reporter should phone you or stop by your work station for information, three general guidelines may be helpful.

Recognize that any conscientious reporter wants to be accurate in gathering and reporting the news but that the limitations imposed by deadlines and work load may prevent absolute accuracy in every detail reported. This leads to the second point.

Try to give to reporters information as complete and accurate as possible, within your area of experience. No reporter will expect you to have information on every aspect of your local government. This leads to the third point.

Encourage the reporter to talk to the mayor, the city or county manager, members of the city council or county board, and department heads. These are the people who can round out the information the reporter needs.

Take pride in your government

Good local government does not just happen. It is created by an informed citizenry, conscientious elected officials and public managers, and dedicated employees working together. You can take pride in being a part of the effort to provide police protection, guard against fire, assess taxes, supply water, maintain streets, educate consumers, care for the elderly, find housing for citizens, and provide many other services to the community.

If you take pride in your government you will want to tell citizens what a good job it is doing. Praise coming directly from an employee can be more effective than a publicity release. It is important that you and your employees be well informed about all aspects of your government and that your facts be correct. After all, the people you talk to will assume you are the expert. And useful information about your government shared with others benefits everyone—the government as well as individual citizens.

Checklist

Provide the best service possible; set the example for your work group.

Be sure your employees know how to do their jobs.

Stay posted on the use of new equipment and new methods for carrying out the work of your unit.

Practice courtesy by letting people know in advance if service is to be interrupted or delayed.

Keep posted on the work of your city or county government so that you can share this information with others.

Know yourself—your appearance, the way you talk, and your behavior.

Keep buildings, grounds, and equipment in good condition.

Avoid taking authorized work breaks in public areas.

Answer questions from the public promptly, courteously, clearly, and accurately.

Review the way you and your employees handle questions and complaints.

Meet with your employees to discuss how to say no in a clear and courteous manner.

Learn the ground rules that news reporters use in gathering and reporting the news.

Take pride in your government! Tell people what you and your fellow workers are doing.

SELECTED BIBLIOGRAPHY

Albanese, Robert. *Management: Toward Accountability for Performance.* Homewood, Ill.: Richard D. Irwin, 1975.

Anderson, Wayne F., et al. *The Effective Local Government Manager.* Washington, D.C.: International City Management Association, 1983.

Arnold, David S., Christine S. Becker, and Elizabeth K. Kellar, eds. *Effective Communication: Getting the Message Across.* Washington, D.C.: International City Management Association, 1983.

Banovetz, James M., ed. *Small Cities and Counties.* Washington, D.C.: International City Management Association, 1984.

Barnard, Chester I. *The Functions of the Executive.* Cambridge, Mass.: Harvard University Press, 1968.

Blake, Robert R., and Jane S. Mouton. *The New Managerial Grid.* Houston: Gulf Publishing, 1978.

Blanchard, Kenneth, and Spencer Johnson. *The One Minute Manager.* New York: Morrow, 1982.

Bolles, Richard Nelson. *The Three Boxes of Life and How to Get Out of Them: An Introduction to Life/Work Planning.* Berkeley, Calif.: Ten Speed Press, 1981.

Burns, James MacGregor. *Leadership.* New York: Harper & Row, 1978.

Cutlip, Scott M., and Allen H. Center. *Effective Public Relations.* 5th ed. Englewood Cliffs, N.J.: Prentice-Hall, 1982.

Drucker, Peter F. *The Effective Executive.* New York: Harper & Row, 1967.

_____. *The Practice of Management.* New York: Harper & Brothers, 1954.

Ends, Earl J., and Curtis W. Page. *Organizational Team Building.* Cambridge, Mass.: Winthrop, 1977.

Gellerman, Saul W. *Management by Motivation.* New York: American Management Association, 1968.

Haney, William V. *Communication and Organizational Behavior: Text and Cases.* 3d ed. Homewood, Ill.: Richard D. Irwin, 1973.

Herzberg, Frederick. *Work and the Nature of Man.* New York: Thomas Y. Crowell, 1966.

Herzberg, Frederick, Bernard Mausner, and Barbara Snyderman. *The Motivation to Work.* New York: John Wiley & Sons, 1967.

Klingner, Donald E. *Public Personnel Management.* Englewood Cliffs, N.J.: Prentice-Hall, 1980.

Kanter, Rosabeth Moss. *The Change Masters.* New York: Simon and Schuster, 1983.

Kellogg, Marion S. *What to Do about Performance Appraisal.* New York: American Management Association, 1975.

Kotter, John P. *Power in Management.* New York: American Management Association, 1979.

Lakein, Alan. *How to Get Control of Your Time and Your Life.* New York: Signet Classics, 1974.

Leavitt, Harold J. *Managerial Psychology.* 4th ed. Chicago: University of Chicago Press, 1978.

Likert, Rensis. *The Human Organization: Its Management and Value.* New York: McGraw-Hill, 1967.

Lincoln, James F. *Incentive Management.* Cleveland, Ohio: Lincoln Electric Company, 1951.

McClelland, David C. *Power: The Inner Experience.* New York: Halsted Press, 1976.

Maccoby, Michael. *The Leader: Managing the Work Place*. New York: Simon and Schuster, 1981.

McConkey, Dale D. *No-Nonsense Delegation*. New York: American Management Association, 1974.

McGregor, Douglas. *The Human Side of Enterprise*. New York: McGraw-Hill, 1960.

Maslow, Abraham H. *Toward a Psychology of Being*. 2d ed. New York: Van Nostrand Reinhold, 1968.

Mintzberg, Henry. *The Nature of Managerial Work*. New York: Harper & Row, 1973.

Morrisey, George L. *Appraisal and Development through Objectives and Results*. Reading, Mass.: Addison-Wesley, 1972.

Naisbitt, John. *Megatrends*. New York: Warner Books, 1982.

Odiorne, George S. *MBO II: A System of Managerial Leadership for the 80's*. Belmont, Calif.: Fearon-Pitman, 1979.

Peters, Thomas J., and Robert H. Waterman, Jr. *In Search of Excellence*. New York: Harper & Row, 1982.

Powers, Stanley Piazza, F. Gerald Brown, and David S. Arnold, eds. *Developing the Municipal Organization*. Washington, D.C.: International City Management Association, 1974.

Reich, Charles A. *The Greening of America*. New York: Random House, 1970.

Reich, Robert B. *The Next American Frontier*. New York: Times Books, 1983.

Sayles, Leonard R. *Leadership: What Effective Managers Really Do . . . and How They Do It*. New York: McGraw-Hill, 1979.

Scandlyn, Sammie Lynn. *101 Winning Ways to Better Municipal Public Relations*. Washington, D.C.: National League of Cities, 1967.

Schein, Edgar H. *Organizational Psychology*. 3d ed. Englewood Cliffs, N.J.: Prentice-Hall, 1980.

Toffler, Alvin. *Future Shock*. New York: Bantam, 1971.

Townsend, Robert. *Up the Organization*. New York: Alfred A. Knopf, 1970.

Yankelovich, Daniel. *New Rules*. New York: Random House, 1981.

Municipal Management Series

Effective
Supervisory
Practices

Text type:

Century Expanded
Helvetica

Composition:

EPS Group Inc.
Baltimore, Maryland

Printing and binding:

Braun-Brumfield, Inc.
Ann Arbor, Michigan

Design:

Herbert Slobin

THE SUPERVISOR'S JOB

1

*The most vital spot
in management
is the point of contact
between
worker and boss*

Lawrence A. Appley

Chapter 1
THE SUPERVISOR'S JOB

Why do we need effective supervisors in local government?

What is the nature of the supervisor's work?

What are the problems of the new supervisor?

What mistakes do new supervisors sometimes make?

What can you do to be a better supervisor?

What has happened in your city or county during the past few years?

Only a short time ago as you looked around, you would almost certainly see new subdivisions, new shopping malls, more streets, perhaps a new city–county complex or sewage treatment plant, new schools. And you were likely to be part of a growing organization. But today in many parts of our country, you are more likely to see closed school buildings, downtowns being revitalized to compete with outlying shopping malls, manufacturing plants temporarily or permanently shut down. Now you may be part of an organization that is struggling to provide even essential public services as your local government attempts to balance its budget with revenue that is barely growing or perhaps even declining in real terms.

Why have these changes taken place? Why have they come about so suddenly and apparently without warning? And what do these changes and those that certainly lie ahead mean for the supervisor in local government?

For almost thirty years after the end of World War II, our country experienced rapid growth. Our population grew rapidly and also became highly mobile. Existing businesses expanded steadily and whole new industries came into being to meet the rising, changing demand for goods and services of our growing, shifting, younger population.

Year after year most people were better off financially than ever before. And since they expected the next year to be even better, they were more and more willing to buy expensive items and to buy on credit. An increasing number of families had two incomes, as one worker took a second job or both husband and wife worked. Two workers in a family often required two cars. Because they could afford to do so, many families moved from rented housing in established neighborhoods into houses of their own in new subdivisions. Then, as their family size and income increased, they moved to larger houses in newer, often suburban neighborhoods. Many families relocated from the Northeast and Midwest to the South and Southwest to take advantage of new and expanding economic opportunities in these rapidly developing parts of our nation. Life styles began to change.

In these new communities, which required water service, sewer lines, sidewalks, and paved streets, the citizens expected and got new schools, more police and fire protection, more parks, playgrounds, and swimming pools as well. During this time of growth and expansion, the federal and state governments provided a great deal of financial aid to local governments.

But then, beginning in the late 1970s, all levels of government began to realize that the money to pay for these new and expanded services, which were getting more expensive every year, was not increasing at the same pace as the demand for these services. Property and other taxes started to rise sharply. As federal, state, and local taxes went up and up, more and more taxpayers found it harder and harder to pay them, because the costs of food, clothing, medical services, and other necessities were soaring also. Citizens began to object to the rising costs of government.

Today, as a result of this sudden turnaround—from a demand for more and better services to a demand for a ceiling on costs—many local governments have had to refocus their efforts. The great need in government today is to manage well the delivery of public services. Cutting back is not the entire answer to today's challenge. Through excellent management of our local governments, we can do more for less—now and in the future.

For reasons that will be explained in Chapter 2, we can be certain that just as supervising in local government today is much different from what it was only a few years ago, the months and years ahead will provide new challenges and opportunities for our cities and counties and, therefore, for supervisors in local government. Tomorrow will be different from today, for we are living in a time of great and rapid change. How do you provide necessary local government services, which cost more each year, without raising taxes—especially property taxes—every year? It takes a well-organized, properly managed local government to do the job. And that kind of organization requires well-organized, highly effective supervisors in every department of local government. It depends on you, working at your best. To help you shoulder this very important responsibility, this chapter explains what your job is, where it begins and ends, and how you can do the kind of job you want to do.

Responsibilities of a supervisor

Five major responsibilities are common to all supervisory jobs:

Getting the job done

Keeping the work area safe and healthy

Encouraging teamwork and cooperation

Developing employee skills

Keeping records and making reports.

Let us take a closer look at each of these responsibilities.

Getting the job done

First and foremost, you are paid to get the work done properly and on time. To accomplish this you have to:

Plan carefully to get the most and the best work done with the least effort and confusion. You need to schedule work so that employees know what they are supposed to do and what results you expect.

Organize workers so they cooperate and work together as a team.

Delegate as much work-related authority as you can, so that employees can develop pride in themselves and in their jobs. They will do a better job if they have responsibility for the work. (But remember that you are still responsible for the results.)

Measure and evaluate the work that you are responsible for. Then you can tell if it is going according to plan and if every member of the work team is doing his or her fair share. You can also catch little mistakes before they grow into big disasters.

Keeping the work area safe and healthy

Accidents are bad news—tragic news if someone is hurt or killed. They not only affect the worker, but can cause suffering and loss for the worker's family as well. And when someone is off the job, that job may not get done. Accidents also mean that insurance rates go up and add to the cost of running local government. Nobody wins; everybody loses.

That is why it is so important to:

Set a personal example by obeying all safety rules yourself and by using safety equipment. By doing so, you also protect yourself and your family.

Plan each job with safety in mind.

Teach safety whenever you teach a worker a new job.

Enforce safety rules at all times—with no exceptions.

Encouraging teamwork

You are responsible not only for the work of those you supervise but also for their attitudes toward work. In fact, you cannot separate the two.

Employees who do good work almost always have high morale and good team spirit. They have common goals and are willing to cooperate to reach those goals. Each person feels he or she is making a contribution to the team. These employees are satisfying their own needs while working toward the goals of the department and the local government. It is up to you to see that your employees work together.

Leading employees includes handling their complaints properly and promptly while maintaining the right kind of discipline in the work group. But getting cooperation in your own unit is not enough. Remember, too, that there are other work groups in your organization: there should be cooperation between your work group and the rest of the management team, as well as between your work group and other work groups in the organization.

Developing employee skills

Start out by believing that most people will surprise you with what they can do if only you will give them a chance. This could mean teaching them a new skill or encouraging them

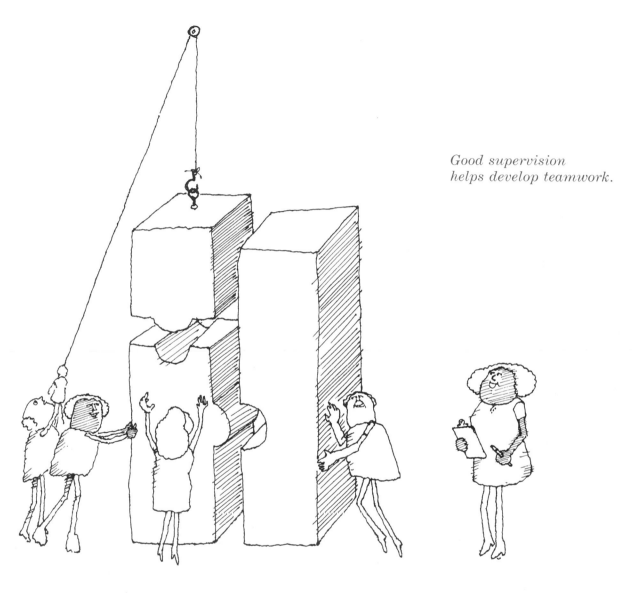

Good supervision helps develop teamwork.

to take on more responsibility. It usually means helping them correct errors, praising their efforts, and recognizing their accomplishments. You are doing some of your best work when you help your employees grow on the job.

Keeping records and making reports

While paperwork may sometimes seem like a chore, there is no way to keep track of your operation without records and reports. It is important to keep your records neatly and accurately and to get your reports in on time. In that way you keep yourself and management in the know and out of trouble.

Duties of a supervisor

Your responsibilities as a supervisor entail, broadly, the following four major duties:

Planning what needs to be done, and by when

Organizing your employees for the job

Developing and maintaining a motivating climate so that employees will be productive

Evaluating how well the job is being done.

The following list will give you a better idea of the specific duties that most local government supervisors have (they are listed at random, not in order of importance):

Explaining policies, procedures, and rules

Planning and scheduling work

Training employees for the job and developing in them a desire to serve the public faithfully and well

Training employees in safety practices

Ensuring that tools and equipment are inspected and properly cared for

Ensuring that materials and equipment are used economically

Getting tools, equipment, and materials to the job site on time

Making work assignments

Getting the right employee on the job at the right time

Controlling accident hazards

Maintaining good housekeeping on the job

Building and maintaining morale

Encouraging teamwork

Settling differences among employees

Improving discipline

Adjusting complaints

Checking and inspecting work

Improving quality and quantity of work

Controlling attendance (absence and tardiness)

Keeping records and making reports

Working cooperatively with other local government departments or offices

Building and maintaining good relations with the public.

The supervisor's place in the organization

Supervisors are vital members of the local government management team. They oversee the individual employee's work and represent the work group on the management team. Indeed, one management expert claims that the supervisor—the point of contact between employees and managers—is at the most vital spot in management.

Because a supervisor is at the same time a member of the local government management team *and* a member of the work team, supervisors often feel conflicting pressures when they try to identify both with man-

Supervisors play a vital role in management through their face-to-face contacts with workers and their linkage with the management above them.

agement and with their work group. Don't be concerned if sometimes you feel caught between the need to satisfy those above you in the organization and your responsibility to represent the needs of your work group. All supervisors sometimes feel this kind of stress. It's just a part of being a supervisor. Truly effective supervisors enjoy the opportunity they have to link their work team into a real, ongoing partnership with the other levels and departments of the local government team.

Your effectiveness as a supervisor is especially important because you meet face to face with your employees every day. Your dealings with them will affect how they feel about management, how willing they are to work, what they think is important to management, how they behave on the job, and how much they grow and develop as persons and as skilled employees.

As a supervisor you have the opportunity to do two things that are vitally important both to your local government and to the other members of your work team. You have the opportunity to be a model for your employees—a leader they can look up to with respect and affection, someone whose behavior they will want to copy. You also have the opportunity as the team leader to be the coach of your work team, helping its members grow and become more skilled and productive as employees, and helping the team become a closely knit, highly effective, and efficient part of your local government.

Problems of the new supervisor

Most of us like the idea of advancing to supervisor. We like the prestige, the authority, the feeling of moving ahead, the recognition of our own good work, and of course the higher pay.

New responsibilities

When you were a worker you may have seen your supervisor riding around in a government car while you were working in the rain, or talking on the phone in a private office while you were pounding a typewriter.

It does not take long, though, to realize that it is not as easy as it looks. From the first day, you are faced with situations that require knowledge, skill, understanding, good judgment, and immediate action. Problems seldom arrive one at a time, and one wrong decision or careless remark can take weeks or months to straighten out. No wonder you sometimes long for the good old days when you did not have to worry about schedules or deadlines, or about workers who were absent or late.

Perhaps it will relieve you to know that the effective supervisors that you see today were themselves originally new and inexperienced. After a period of adjustment they came to enjoy their work and to find it satisfying to be effective supervisors.

Common mistakes

Before they reach that point, however, many new supervisors seem to make similar mistakes and to encounter similar problems. Perhaps reading about them here will help you avoid these mistakes.

When you were a worker instead of a supervisor, you had only your own work to think about. Now you are responsible for seeing that others do their work. It is important to remember that your job is now to supervise this work, not to do it yourself. But many new supervisors find it hard to shift from *doing* the work to *supervising* it. They know as much about the work as the employees do—or perhaps more—but they are not sure what a supervisor is supposed to do, especially if they have not received any training. Thus, they spend most of their day doing what the employees should be doing, or looking over the employees' shoulders.

Another mistake of some new supervisors is to let authority go to their heads—to act as though they are better than the employees and to pull rank, order people around, and let everyone know they are "the boss."

Most employees will either laugh at such supervisors (behind their backs, of course) or will become resentful and stay out of their way. These supervisors thereby lose touch with their employees.

Other supervisors may swing too far in the opposite direction. They may try to keep up the "buddy" kind of friendship they may have had with their fellow workers before they were promoted. The new supervisor should realize that he or she must balance on a fine line—somewhere between being one of the gang and being the one in charge.

Both you and your workers must understand at the outset that you are not just another worker. You are the supervisor, with all the authority and responsibility that go with the job. At the same time, though, it is important to show by your actions that you are concerned about your employees and that you are working together with them toward agreed-upon goals.

Toward better supervision

As a manager, the supervisor should be able to get work done through others. This means you, as supervisor, should organize work and motivate employees so that they will do what they are required to do voluntarily.

If you want to test your ability to do this, find out whether your employees work as hard when you are away as when you are there. Only willing, well-supervised employees work hard when the supervisor's back is turned. Your job will be more rewarding—and you will become more valuable to your organization—if you use management skills to make your work easier and more effective.

Getting work done through others

Getting work done through the efforts of others is not as easy today as it used to be. In the so-called "good old days" an employee either worked hard or was fired. In some jobs the supervisor was the man who could "lick every other man on his crew"—and did, if the worker did not do as he was told. Although time has added a legendary gloss to those railroad, steel mill, and packinghouse foremen, there remains a substantial element of truth to their awesome powers of hiring, disciplining, and firing workers.

But times have changed. Today's workers, particularly younger ones, require a different type of supervising. The work-pusher type of supervisor cannot survive when workers are protected by civil service provisions, union contracts, grievance procedures, antidiscrimination laws, and the willingness of workers to go to court to protect their rights. And employees today have a sense of these rights and of their worth as individual men and women.

Today's employees respond willingly to leaders whom they respect and admire. A good beginning is to try asking your workers for advice or help. Ask them to help you plan what needs to be done and how best to do it. Let them have a voice in deciding how to organize to get the job done.

Individuals and small groups can be remarkably effective at planning, organizing, and carrying through on specific assignments. The gains in productivity and work quality can be impressive, and the employees will take great pride in *their* achievements.

Get to know your workers. Find out each person's strengths and weaknesses. Try to learn what each person wants and needs to get from his or her job. By your actions let your employees know that you have confidence in their ability and trust them to do things the right way.

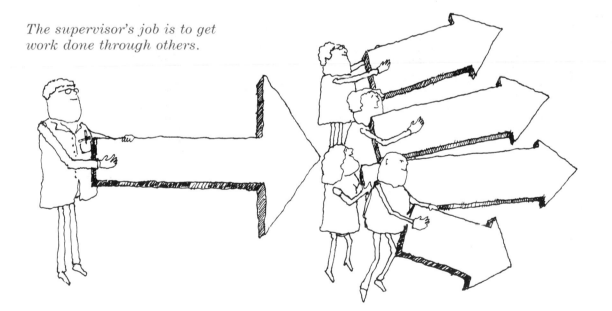

The supervisor's job is to get work done through others.

Treating employees fairly

Treat everyone fairly. It is important to avoid playing favorites and to be consistent in your behavior. You lose credibility if you are standoffish one day and everyone's "pal" the next.

Above all, do not let your personal beliefs interfere with your decisions as a supervisor.

Let us take a closer look at this point. As a citizen, you have a perfect right to your views about what is right and wrong, good and bad. Under the law, however, we cannot practice those beliefs that limit the rights of others. As a supervisor, then, you cannot treat employees differently because of their race, religion, nationality, sex, or age.

Regardless of your own opinions, your employees are guaranteed equal opportunity by law. If you violate their rights as citizens or violate the equal opportunity laws, you can be sued and made to pay damages out of your own pocket; in addition, such a violation could cause serious problems for your local government.

It is important to be fair with your workers in still another way: Remember that you have authority over them *only* during working hours; you *do not* have authority over their private lives or what they do on their own time.

If your local government has rules about appropriate dress, your employees should dress accordingly. But you may not add your personal requirements to those regulations. If the requirement is for neatly groomed hair, you cannot add to that your own preference for short hair. If an employee drinks off the job but has a good attendance record and is always sober at work, then that drinking has nothing to do with his or her job or with your job as supervisor.

Remember, too, that giving workers advice about their personal problems—even if they ask for it—can be a mistake. You should concern yourself with an employee's private life *only* when it affects job performance. This does not mean that you should not be willing to *listen* to employees with personal problems. Listening to your employees when they want to talk about their problems helps you to understand them better. It also improves relationships and communication between you and your employees. It is important to know, however, when and how to advise an employee to get professional help, instead of trying to solve a problem yourself.

In any situation in which you suspect that your personal preferences or an employee's personal life may be involved, it is important to ask yourself, "Does this have anything to do with the employee's job performance?" before you do or say anything. You can get into serious trouble if you use your supervisory authority to regulate or influence an employee's behavior outside of working hours.

Summary

Why should you look so carefully at the duties and responsibilities of a supervisor's job? You should do so because effective supervision depends on every part of that job.

Some supervisors are so intent on production that they overlook safety or training. Some supervisors neglect records and reports, while others give too much time to paperwork. Some supervisors become so concerned with people that they neglect work. All of us have parts of our jobs that we like much better than other parts. The trouble starts when as supervisors we pay too much attention to some parts of our job and neglect others.

We should strive for balanced supervision. This means that the effective supervisor will put proper emphasis on each responsibility and duty.

And we should always remember that an effective supervisor is not a person with special personality traits and unusual skills. Research tells us that all a supervisor has to do to become highly effective at supervision is to learn how to behave like an effective supervisor. These behaviors can be learned, and they will be discussed in the chapters that follow.

Checklist

Be a leader, not a boss.

Ask your workers to help you plan what to do and how to do it.

Ask your workers for advice and help in getting the job done.

Let your workers help decide how to organize their work.

Show confidence in your employees' judgment by letting them make some of the decisions, but remember you are still responsible for the work they do.

Be sure that everyone knows the what, how, and when of every major task.

Get to know your workers; learn what they need and what they can contribute.

Build teamwork among all the persons in your organization.

Teach and enforce health and safety rules, and set a good personal example.

Keep your records and reports accurately and neatly, and get them in on time.

Try to be a teacher, a helper, and a leader—not a tough boss or a lenient buddy.

Treat everyone fairly. Since everyone is different, however, remember that treating everyone in exactly the same way may be unfair to some.

Do not allow your personal beliefs to interfere with your treatment of employees or your job decisions.

Do not interfere in the private lives of your employees.

Remember that your job is to get work done through others.

THE SUPERVISOR AND THE CHANGING ENVIRONMENT

To survive, the individual must become infinitely more adaptable and capable than ever before

Alvin Toffler

Chapter 2
THE SUPERVISOR AND
THE CHANGING ENVIRONMENT

What is happening in our country and in the world around us that is changing your job as supervisor?

Why and in what ways are today's employees different from employees of the previous generation?

Can a supervisor be made to pay damages personally for wrongful actions that are job-connected?

How should today's employees be supervised?

If you had left your job in 1940 and returned in 1950, things probably would have been much the same as when you left. But if you left your job today and came back ten years from now, you would probably be startled by how much had changed.

Exactly the same is true of our communities, our country, and the world in general. A number of powerful forces are rapidly changing the world around us and the attitudes of many of us toward life and work. These forces affect the values and behavior of today's workers and have caused the supervisor's job—your job—to change as well.

These forces include the following:

The tremendous growth in world population

Major changes in the economy of our country

A major shifting of our population—from central cities to suburbs and previously rural areas; and from the North to the South, particularly the Southwest

The high percentages of older people and young adults in our population and in the work force, and the impact of a new "baby boom"

The impact of computers and the development of the "information society"

New laws and court decisions about basic rights of citizens.

Changes in our world and our country

Let us look first at the big changes that are taking place in the world around us and in our country—then at how they are affecting the way employees think and behave. Then we can look at how the supervisor's job has changed, and what the supervisor must do to continue to supervise effectively.

Increased population since 1850

Just about 135 years ago, in 1850, there were approximately a billion people on the earth. Today, it is estimated that there are more than 4.5 billion. By the turn of the century, there probably will be about 6.5 billion, and less than a hundred years from now, some 12 billion.

You can see very clearly how rapidly the world's population is growing if you look at the number of years it has taken to add each billion people to the population of the earth. It took many centuries for that population to reach one billion, but only 80 years to add a second billion, 31 years to reach three billion, and then only 14 years to add a fourth billion.

What does this rapid growth in the world's population mean for local government? Some experts think it means continued inflation for our country and, therefore, rising costs for local government. Remember that there is only so much gas and oil, iron ore, coal, and other natural resources in our planet. Two or three or four times as many people as before demanding to use resources means that prices are likely to rise. Food prices also are likely to rise as a growing world population requires two or three or four times as much food as was needed before.

The population of the United States has increased by approximately 90 million people since World War II. That amounts to the combined populations of California, Florida, Illinois, Michigan, New Jersey, New York, and Pennsylvania. By the year 2000 we probably will have added another 40 million, to make a total of almost 270 million Americans—nearly twice as many as there were in 1945.

This population growth is one reason why local governments expanded so rapidly during the 1950s, 1960s and the early 1970s. And since our population is still growing, though less rapidly than before, the demand for essential local government services will continue to grow. Population growth also means that many people will be living and working under more crowded conditions, while others will be moving as far away from the crowding as they are able.

What does this have to do with you, the supervisor? It means that you will have to deal with some of the problems that grow out of greater crowding on and off the job. Some of you who supervise in areas of continued population growth probably will be working in larger departments and larger local governments. Many of you whose departments and local governments are not growing may experience some of the problems associated with crowding on the job as your cost-conscious local governments strive to be more efficient and economical in using space. Research tells us that crowding tends to lead to behavior problems—problems may arise

from crowding on the job or workers may bring stress-related problems with them to the job.

In a larger organization workers often feel like small cogs on a large wheel and they need large doses of recognition and responsibility to help them feel important. Today's younger employers, who have grown up with about 90 million more people than their parents did, sometimes feel that their names are not as important as their social security numbers (and they may be right). They may feel that larger organizations do not see them as human beings or as individuals but only as "hands" or "personnel" or "employees."

Many have grown up in crowded cities or in suburbs where the population was highly mobile and where they did not get to know their neighbors and their neighbors did not get to know them. Many have no deep roots in a community as their parents and grandparents probably did, because their families moved from place to place while they were growing up.

Today's workers also differ from their counterparts of a generation ago in that they are likely to be better educated, more independent, more assertive, and more inquisitive—and to expect more of their society. They want to participate, be important, and be involved. In other words, they expect and demand "a piece of the action." All of this means that supervisors need to give em-

ployees the opportunity to be distinctive, to have a sense of belonging at work. It is important for supervisors to make sure that each employee is part of his or her work team and that the morale of the team is high.

The growth of metropolitan America

In 1800 only 6 percent of the people in the United States lived in cities (as defined by

In 1800 almost everyone—94 percent of the population—lived in rural areas. By 1980, 74 percent were living in cities, towns, and other urban areas.

In 1980, 26 percent of the
population was rural. Most
of these people commuted to
the city or town for
nonfarm employment.

the Census Bureau). The rest of the population lived in rural areas and was mostly engaged in farming. By 1980 the Census Bureau reported that 74 percent of our population was living in cities, towns, and other "urban" areas. Of the 26 percent classified as rural in 1980, less than 2.5 percent lived on farms. Most of the workers in the rural population commute to cities, towns, and other population centers for nonfarm employment.

It is expected that by the year 2000 an even smaller percentage of the population will live in rural areas. By that time about 30 million more people probably will have moved to, or be surrounded by, subdivisions and suburbs built on what is rural land today.

You can see why local government will be growing in some areas, declining in some areas, and changing the kinds of public services provided in other areas.

Major economic changes

In 1950, 65 percent of U.S. workers were employed as laborers in industry. Today, that percentage has dropped to about 30 percent as our economy has undergone a restructuring. Many experts say that our nation is in a major transition—from a manufacturing society that produces automobiles, steel, appliances, textiles, clothing, and shoes to an "information society," manufacturing and servicing computers, designing computer software, and developing and operating chains of financial services "supermarkets." More than half of American workers today are employed in creating, processing, and transmitting information.

Major population shifts

In addition to the shifts of population from farms, rural areas, and central cities to suburban areas, yet another major shifting of our population is under way. This shift is associated with the major restructuring of our national economy. Manufacturing plants must be located near adequate supplies of labor, water, and raw materials such as coal, and near transportation centers. Information companies can locate almost anywhere, and what they tend to look for in deciding where to locate is the quality of life in a community—climate, education systems, cultural attractiveness, availability of recreational areas. Reflecting these factors, about 90 percent of growth in our country—population and economic—is occurring in the Southwest and in Florida.

More older and younger people in the work force

Before the 1930s families in this country often had four or more children. But during the Great Depression of the 1930s families could not afford many children. Also, when families moved from farms to cities they did not need as many children. On a farm, children were extra pairs of hands; in the city, they were extra mouths to feed.

After World War II, in the late 1940s, a baby boom began. It lasted more than fifteen years—into the early 1960s.

The result of these changes in family size, and of advances in medicine that have steadily increased life spans, is a population that looks like this in the 1980s:

Large numbers of young adults in their twenties and thirties, born during the baby boom of the late 1940s, the 1950s, and the early 1960s

A smaller percentage than usual of adults in their forties and early fifties, born during the Depression and war years, when birthrates were low

A growing number of older persons, fifty-five years of age and up, who were born before the Depression, when families were larger. This group is growing in number because of increasing longevity.

Today young adults make up close to half of the typical work force. Born during or after World War II, they tend to have attitudes and values somewhat different from those of their parents, especially about work and authority.

The result of all these changes is that additional responsibilities are placed on the supervisor—to understand the ideas and attitudes of both older and younger workers, and to blend different values and attitudes into a working whole.

Looking ahead as members of the local government's management team, you need to be aware that our nation soon will be moving into a period of labor shortage. Those Americans who were born at the end of the post–World War II baby boom now either are in or will soon be entering the labor market. Behind them, representing the source of new and replacement employees, are the smaller and smaller numbers born as our national birthrate declined from 1962 through 1975—the period of the "baby bust." We have seen this decline in birthrate reflected earlier in smaller enrollments in our elementary schools, many of which were closed during the mid- and later 1970s. During the 1980s, the number of Americans under age twenty will fall to the lowest percentage of the population in our history. A recent study by a highly respected research organization indicates that in the not-too-distant future the United States may have to import people from outside the country to meet our need for workers.

Furthermore, new changes in the age distribution pattern of our population may lie ahead, as a new baby boom seems now to be under way. Our national birthrate has been rising since the fall of 1976.

*The impact of computers
and the "explosion of knowledge"*

Without doubt, our local governments are already significantly affected by the greatly increased use of ever more sophisticated computers. There are now a half-billion more computers in the world than there are human beings.

Also, as almost 90 percent of the scientists who have ever lived are still alive today—their scientific efforts greatly aided by computers—our knowledge of nearly every field, subject, and phase of life is racing ahead as never before. One expert has suggested that, whereas it took about 1,750 years—from the birth of Christ almost up to the American Revolution—for mankind's knowledge to double, the most recent doubling of our knowledge and information has taken only about 4 years.

This means that if you were in school between 1930 and 1950, let us say, and if you have not done much reading since and have not had much on-the-job training, you will probably have missed a lot of the knowledge explosion that those you supervise under the age of thirty-five have experienced.

It is obvious that keeping up-to-date has become increasingly important. This is a challenge to the employees on your work team and should be an even greater challenge to you as their supervisor.

Both you and your employees, then, must be ready for change and for progress. It is important that you encourage employees to learn more about the work they do, that you train them in new ideas and new methods, and that you help them to keep up with new developments and to understand that new developments can change the nature of a job or do away with a job entirely. Beyond that, it is important for you and for them to understand that change is normal—especially today—and may be a very good thing.

It must be said that the person who stands still on the job or insists on doing everything in the old way may be in danger of being replaced by a more adaptable worker, or possibly by a computer.

Above all, it is important that you as supervisor keep up-to-date yourself. You can learn from your younger workers or from other associates who may have been in school more recently. You can also learn from those who have had special training that you have not had. Take time to read, to think, and to question.

Laws and court decisions

Since the mid-1960s Congress has passed numerous laws covering civil rights and discrimination, consumer protection, the environment, worker safety and health, and privacy of citizens. In addition, citizen rights under the U.S. Constitution are being more vigorously enforced than was the case a few years ago. For example, while in 1960 there were only 247 civil rights suits in federal courts against government officials, by 1979 there were nearly 25,000 such lawsuits. From the point of view of the supervisor the most important of these laws and decisions are those pertaining to citizen rights, particularly in these areas:

Freedom of speech

The right to assemble peaceably and to petition the government for correction of grievances

The rights of blacks, Hispanics, and other minority citizens

Protection against unlawful searches of people or property and unlawful seizure of personal belongings

The right to due process of law

The right to equal treatment regardless of sex

The right to equal employment treatment for those forty to seventy years of age.

These laws mean that all people have specific rights as citizens. Most of these rights are spelled out in the Bill of Rights to the U.S. Constitution. All citizens have these rights in equal amounts, whether they are white, black, Hispanic, Eskimo, American Indian, or any other race or ethnic group.

These basic rights belong to men and women; Protestants, Catholics, Jews, and atheists; citizens born in this country and abroad. They apply regardless of whether your family came from England, Poland, Italy, Mexico, or New Jersey.

It is important that supervisors be aware of the rights people have under the law. A local government can be sued and made to pay damages if found guilty of violating federal law. A supervisor, too, can be sued and made to pay damages if found guilty of depriving another person of his or her legal rights. *You,*

We live with a tidal wave of information. Your ability to navigate will determine your ability to succeed.

personally, can be sued in these cases—even if you, the supervisor, were acting according to state law, local ordinance, or departmental rule.

Here are two examples of how you, a supervisor, might get into trouble with the law. Let us suppose you are a lieutenant in the fire department and a woman is sent to you to be interviewed for a job. You have decided long ago that a woman can never meet the demands of firefighter jobs, so you reject her application without talking to her or giving her a chance to show what she can do.

If you reject this application only because she is a woman, you could be in trouble. The law says you may not discriminate against any applicant just because that person is older, is a woman, is black, is Hispanic, or whatever. You may turn down only applicants who do not have the qualifications for the job. Of course, if you *do* hire the applicant *only* because the applicant is a woman or is black, you may be in trouble, too, unless that person is the best qualified applicant.

Let us take another example. Assume that you give an order to a worker on the job. The worker does what he is told to do, but he also tells you a few unflattering things you do not like to hear. You fire him on the spot.

You may be in trouble again—this time for violating the employee's rights to free speech and due process of law. If an employee refuses to obey your proper instructions, you may discipline the employee for disobeying. You may as a supervisor have cause to discipline an employee for sounding off, but you could get into trouble for firing someone for exercising free speech or for firing someone without properly informing that person of the reason and giving that person a chance to tell his or her side.

The way to handle such a situation is to take the case through the proper disciplinary channels, described in Chapter 13. Both you and the employee are allowed to state your case. You have to prove that what the employee said seriously interfered with proper discipline, and the employee is able to present his or her side.

In short, as a supervisor you should respect the constitutional and statutory rights of everyone you work with; and following good supervisory practices will help you to do that.

New attitudes toward life and work

For many years most Americans believed in and lived by what is called the Protestant ethic. Many of us still do. This is a set of values and beliefs that emphasizes hard work, standing on your own feet, thrift, saving for a rainy day, knowing your place, and obeying anyone who is older or has higher rank. Rest, vacations, and leisure are earned—they are the rewards of hard work.

Today many Americans—especially many of those under thirty-five—live by a different set of values. It is sometimes called the "psychology of entitlement" because its followers believe that people are entitled to certain basic necessities, such as a decent job and dignified retirement, decent housing, medical care, a clean environment, and safe consumer products.

Leisure is also considered by many to be a right rather than a privilege earned by work. One way of seeing how our values and attitudes are changing, for example, is to compare some typical attitudes and values from our past with those that many people are embracing and expressing today.

Yesterday's employees lived to work. They wanted to get and keep good jobs because they remembered the Great Depression. A good job was any job that offered job security and a pension for their old age. The possibility of another depression was always in the back of their minds. They saved faithfully for "a rainy day" and they paid off their mortgages as quickly as possible.

But many workers today are not preoccupied with financial security. Younger employees are more likely to work to live. The Great Depression, with its widespread bankruptcies and enduring bread lines, has little or no meaning for them. Of course, the deep recession of the early 1980s may have had an impact on the values of some of these

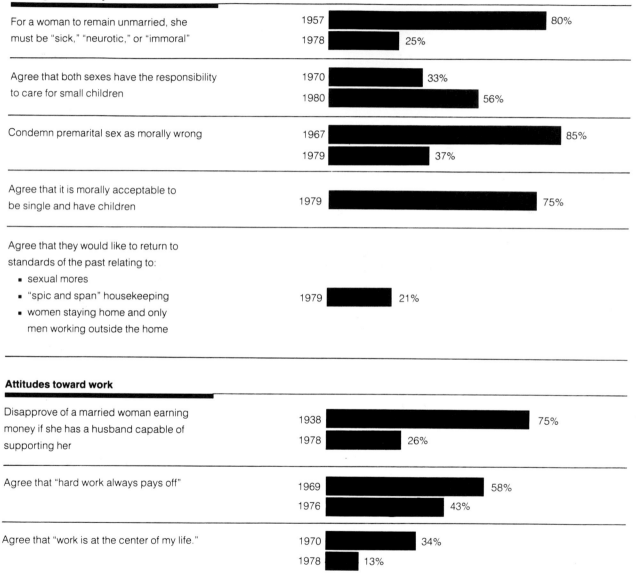

CHANGING SOCIAL VALUES AND ATTITUDES TOWARD WORK

Marriage and family

For a woman to remain unmarried, she must be "sick," "neurotic," or "immoral"
- 1957 — 80%
- 1978 — 25%

Agree that both sexes have the responsibility to care for small children
- 1970 — 33%
- 1980 — 56%

Condemn premarital sex as morally wrong
- 1967 — 85%
- 1979 — 37%

Agree that it is morally acceptable to be single and have children
- 1979 — 75%

Agree that they would like to return to standards of the past relating to:
- sexual mores
- "spic and span" housekeeping
- women staying home and only men working outside the home
- 1979 — 21%

Attitudes toward work

Disapprove of a married woman earning money if she has a husband capable of supporting her
- 1938 — 75%
- 1978 — 26%

Agree that "hard work always pays off"
- 1969 — 58%
- 1976 — 43%

Agree that "work is at the center of my life."
- 1970 — 34%
- 1978 — 13%

younger workers. But approximately 90 percent of workers were not personally unemployed and many of those who were may feel even more strongly that they are "entitled" to a decent job. Besides, today's employees have social security for their families if they die or become disabled and for themselves in their old age (although many younger workers now question whether social security benefits will be available to them when they retire). Almost anywhere today's employees work they will have a pension plan plus medical and life insurance. If they lose their jobs they can expect unemployment compensation. Therefore, you do not hear as much talk as in the past about rainy days or nest eggs.

But you probably do hear quite a lot about people doing their thing, because many of today's younger workers believe in it—in the chance to be themselves, to develop their own special set of talents. They also want their lives, including their work, to be interesting and meaningful.

Today's employees realize that while they are decision makers in their homes, their churches, their clubs, and their voting booths,

Source: Daniel Yankelovich, *New Rules: Searching for Self-Fulfillment in a World Turned Upside Down* (New York: Random House, 1981), 93-96.

this is often not true at work where they spend about a quarter of their lives. Many of them speak openly of their resentment and anger at having very little say about how they should do their jobs. And when employers deny today's workers what they need and want from their jobs, many will not hesitate to fight back. In local government they may "fight back" by joining a union. In fact, about 20 percent of all local and state government employees now belong to unions.

Many of today's employees do not believe that hard work pays off. Many value their leisure more than their working hours. And many tend to feel that they have a right to time off. If such a person does not feel like working on Monday, he or she might not come to work.

Finally, today's younger, better educated and more assertive worker is less likely to say to supervisors or top management, "O.K. if you say so." Instead, many may reply to a direction or suggestion, "Why?" or, "Why not?"

What is expected of today's supervisor?

Today's effective supervisor recognizes the reality of the new values and attitudes and tries to find ways of effectively dealing with all employees—ways that are acceptable to *them*. This means building good relations with employees and strengthening their willingness to work harder and better. Remember that those employees who embrace the newer attitudes toward life and work are *not* less motivated than workers who believe in the work ethic. It is just that they have higher expectations from their work, and for them work has to compete more directly with other values in their lives.

To build good relations with employees and strengthen their willingness to work harder and better, today's supervisor must have a greater appreciation of how complex human beings are and a better understanding of what makes them tick and how they relate to the changing world around them. The supervisor must be able to sense and adapt to the changes in employee needs—from time to time and from situation to situation. And today's supervisor must be both patient and reasonable. If you push today's younger employees, many are likely to push back, aware of their rights under the law.

Following are techniques that should serve as useful rules to follow in supervising today's employees.

Anticipate and plan

Today's supervisor spends more time thinking about tomorrow's problems and planning for them. Changes are easier and smoother for the work team if the supervisor has anticipated what is coming and has planned for it. Since changes are happening at a faster pace in the world, changes can be expected to happen faster on the job, too.

Help employees set goals

Today's supervisor helps workers identify their goals. Supervisors need to help workers find ways of satisfying their own needs and meeting the goals of the organization at the same time.

Make employees part of the work team

Today's supervisor finds ways of making each employee a part of his or her work team, of giving each employee a sense of belonging.

Keep employees up-to-date

Today's supervisor gives the growth and development of employees top priority, keeping them from being narrow specialists by enriching their jobs, providing them with the broadest possible range of skills, and seeing that they are kept up-to-date.

Give employees responsibility and the authority to carry out that responsibility

Today's supervisor gives greater work-related responsibility and delegates more authority. By bringing employees into the planning process and by putting more trust in them, supervisors can challenge employees to do their very best.

*America still is a mobile society. We
are moving minds to information centers.
You are hiring minds (not arms and backs)
that are attracted to the quality of life
you can offer.*

Show respect for employees

Today's supervisor shows that he or she respects the employees. For example, the supervisor addresses employees by name and never uses "boy," "my girl," or "hey, you."

Encourage employees to speak up

Today's supervisor encourages employees to provide information and suggestions, or to pose questions or problems. The supervisor encourages employees to express resentment, complaints, or differences of opinion. If a worker tells off a supervisor, the effective supervisor remains calm, knowing the worker may be right and that supervisors can learn, as well.

Listen to employees

Today's supervisor listens carefully to employees and tries to understand, giving employees the same attention the supervisor would expect from his or her own superior. Suggestions or questions are followed up with a report. "I'll check on that and let you know by Friday." And the effective supervisor does report back, by Friday.

Checklist

Be aware of those changes in our society that have had or are likely to have an impact on your organization.

Be aware of the technological advances that are now affecting your local government and its employees.

Be sensitive to employee needs for a sense of responsibility, of individuality, of belonging.

Keep up-to-date on the advances in technology and other fields of knowledge affecting your work.

Be fully aware of all your employees' rights as citizens.

Maintain an understanding of the values and attitudes of younger and "new breed" workers as well as those of older and more traditional workers.

BASIC
SUPERVISORY
SKILLS

The science of management is a thoughtful, organized, and human approach to the performance of the management job

Lawrence A. Appley

Chapter 3
BASIC SUPERVISORY SKILLS

**How can you prevent trouble
before it starts?**

**How can you be sure your workers
get their work done?**

How can you get workers to pull together?

**How can you give workers leeway
without losing control?**

**Is a supervisor always the leader
of the work group?**

**How can you get workers to work willingly
and well on their own?**

**How can you get an average group
to turn out excellent work?**

Food experts tell us that a balanced diet contains at least one item from each of four basic food groups—every day. Learning how to cook and serve these foods is important, too, but you must start with the right kinds of food.

In the same way, management has its basics. These are seven fundamental skills or competencies that supervisors must develop to do an effective job. Later chapters will give you more specific recipes for putting these basic skills to work. Now, however, we should talk about these seven skills, which are basic to the kind of effective supervising you want to do, namely:

Stopping problems before they get out of hand

Setting goals and reaching them

Building a team and keeping it going

Giving workers a say about their jobs

Being a leader as well as a supervisor

Making jobs more interesting and rewarding

Coaching workers to improve their skills.

Understanding the meaning of and reasons for these essentials of good management gives the supervisor a firm foundation on which to build more specific skills and a good work organization.

Stopping problems before they get out of hand

Effective supervisors watch for small signs of trouble so as to deal with them before they grow into serious problems

To catch a problem while it is still a small one, you will have to develop a kind of sixth sense, or an early warning system, which alerts you to trouble ahead. Most of us use a sixth sense in personal situations. It tells you that the friend you are with is feeling a lot worse than she admits; that your son is embarrassed even though he is acting cocky; that your wife or husband is thinking about something else while you are talking; or that the other poker player has a very good hand.

In all these cases we are observing small clues in a person's face or voice or posture that tell us to be on guard. In the same way we can learn to be observant at work. Supervisors who genuinely like the members of their work team and are sensitive to their feelings will probably be able to sense when a problem is beginning to develop.

Keeping one step ahead of trouble also means being able to see trends or patterns in the clues that you notice. For example, if a usually cooperative worker suddenly becomes difficult to work with, that is a clue telling you that there may be trouble ahead. But if other workers who are usually friendly begin looking away when you pass by, a *pattern* of trouble may be developing. You can assume that the problem involves more than one worker and that it is a lot more serious than it may have looked at first.

Your early warning signals can come from your employees or from other people in your organization, as well as from people outside of local government. Supervisors who are approachable, whose supervisory style makes people tend to confide in them and talk frankly with them, who maintain good relations with everyone inside and outside the organization—these supervisors have the best chance of getting help in anticipating problems.

It is an early warning signal when workers in your group exclude you.

For example, one of your employees may tell you that repair work on your vehicles is not being done properly. You would then be able to take action before a breakdown or a serious accident occurs. Or a neighbor who knows and respects you might alert you to the fact that one of your employees is offering items for sale which might be local government property. You could then check the facts and take corrective action if necessary before a mistake turns into a scandal.

Anticipating problems means more than simply being the kind of supervisor that people find it easy to talk to. It also means being a supervisor who has budgeted the time to gather information, to think, and to plan.

Setting goals and reaching them

The second basic skill a supervisor must have is the ability to pinpoint *what* must be done, *when*, and *by whom*. In other words, supervisors must be able to set goals and state them clearly.

Setting clear goals

A goal is frequently called an objective or, sometimes, a target. In any case, it is an exact statement of what must be done and when it must be completed. Here, for instance, is an example of a goal statement: Crew 1 is to complete properly all curb and gutter work on the north side of the 1400 block of Oak Street no later than 4:30 P.M. on Friday, 15 November.

This statement gives the supervisor and the workers the specific goal that must be reached. It also gives everyone an exact deadline for getting the job done. This is much more effective than simply urging employees to work harder and faster, as some supervisors do. The clearer the idea that workers have of what they are supposed to do, the greater the possibility of its getting done.

There is another good reason for stating goals clearly. Goals are needed because progress can only be measured if we know exactly what the group is moving toward. In other words, the players cannot tell when they have scored if there is no goal line. For example, if the curb and gutter work is not completed on time, the supervisor and workers should get together to figure out why. Was the deadline too short? Did the workers let the supervisor down? Was equipment late in arriving? Once the reason is found, it will be easier to do a better job of planning the next time.

Setting goals does not mean simply stating what the next work order on the pile requires the work crew to do. Before a goal is stated, supervisors should think through which job *should* be next in line. Priorities must be set so that work is done in order of importance, with the most important job placed at the top of the list.

In addition, tasks can often be grouped so that similar work is done together or con-

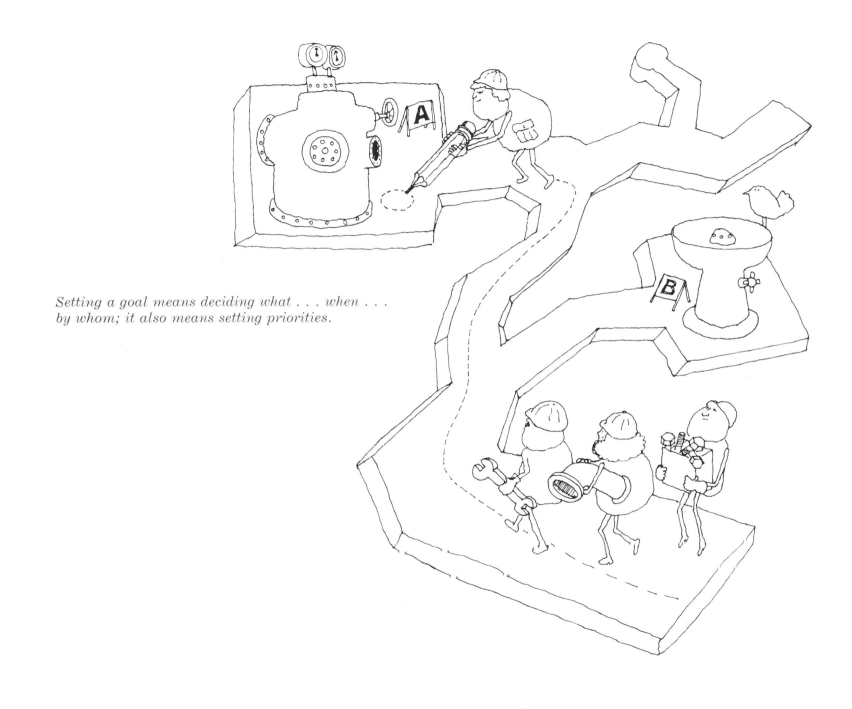

Setting a goal means deciding what . . . when . . .
by whom; it also means setting priorities.

secutively. Time and materials can often be saved by grouping work elements in this way, and the work crew is thus working more efficiently.

While the most effective managers work closely with their supervisors in setting work goals, the goals of a work team sometimes are determined by management at higher levels of the department or local government. When goals assigned to the work team seem unrealistic or inappropriate to those closest to the job, effective supervisors strive to influence management to set more realistic or appropriate goals. They try to help the higher levels of the organization understand the realities of the work situation by providing timely and accurate information.

Building personal goals into organizational goals

The supervisor who recognizes that workers have goals of their own, and who tries to help workers reach these goals, has gone a long way toward getting employees to work willingly and well.

At work, personal goals might be getting promoted or earning more pay. But many personal goals have to do with an employee's interests outside the job, such as going hunting, doing Christmas shopping, or painting a room in one's house.

Many of you can remember the days when sanitation workers were required to return to the public works department after garbage and trash were collected, to sit idly around until the workday was over. Now, in many local governments, supervisors are authorized to allow the workers to go home when the collection routes have been satisfactorily completed. The workers have properly accomplished the goals of their local government and are free to go about accomplishing their personal goals, whatever those might be. Under such an arrangement workers are strongly motivated to work both quickly and well. As a supervisor, perhaps you don't have this kind of authority delegated to you. But when you *are* able to bring the organization's goals and the employees' personal goals together, the result is motivation. This result is most easily obtained by supervisors who encourage employees to help in planning and setting goals for their work team.

Building a team and keeping it going

Some supervisors only give orders to their *subordinates*, others head work *groups*. But the most effective supervisors are leaders of closely knit work *teams*. A group is simply a collection of individuals, but a team is something more. It is a group of people who trust one another and count on each and every member to help with the work. They share the same values; they have a team spirit.

Team spirit grows out of the same feeling of pride and belonging that people get from being members of a championship athletic team, a lodge or sorority, or a crack military unit. We usually give more of ourselves to organizations that have team spirit than we do to other groups we belong to.

When a group of workers becomes a true team, two important things take place. First, the workers gain the sense of belonging mentioned above. Second, the whole becomes greater than the sum of its parts. This means that a team of people working together can get more done than the members of the team could accomplish working individually.

But teams must be built; and once built they must be maintained. Like a fine piece of machinery, unless they are handled carefully and given preventive maintenance they will break down.

Giving workers a say about their jobs

The supervisor should recognize that an employee who is doing a job eight hours a day, five days a week, twelve months a year, knows more about that job than the supervisor does. The supervisor may have been an expert at the same work some time ago, but since he or she became a supervisor he or she has probably not actually patrolled a beat or posted entries in the account books.

Your workers, then, may be the best sources for ideas on how to perform their jobs—and how to **perform these jobs most effectively, efficiently, and economically**. And employees whose supervisors seek their advice on these jobs will generally perform well because they have a sense of "ownership" in their work and they feel that their knowledge of the job is valued.

Delegating is managing through others

When you delegate authority for work and accept the decisions workers make about how best to do their jobs you are truly managing through the efforts of others. Such a relationship helps the supervisor become the leader of the team rather than the boss of the work group.

Delegating authority to employees also makes their jobs more interesting and helps them to grow and develop. Finally, delegating authority gives the supervisor the most effective control he or she can have: self-control on the part of the workers themselves. When self-control is operating, then employees are doing what needs to be done even when the supervisor is not present.

Delegation is not loss of authority

Many supervisors find it hard to delegate authority because they are afraid of losing control. If they understood the true meaning of delegation they would see that this does not, in fact, happen.

A supervisor does not delegate his or her authority as a supervisor. Supervisors always retain the authority delegated to them

by management—the authority to decide what work must be done, in what order of importance, when, at what level of quality, and by whom.

True delegation involves giving workers *only authority related to work*—authority to decide *how* the work should be done. Besides, this authority is delegated only to employees who have demonstrated that they are experts at their jobs.

If employees do not have the knowledge or skills to make proper decisions about how their jobs should be done, the supervisor should first train them and then work with them to improve their skills and abilities. Work authority can then be delegated increasingly to these workers as the supervisor becomes satisfied that they can make proper decisions on their own.

Being a leader as well as a supervisor

As a supervisor you have what is called the formal authority that goes with your position—the authority that is assigned to you by your superiors. In other words, you are a supervisor because top management has made you one.

You probably also have the authority which is based on your knowledge of what is done in your work unit—the authority of an expert. When something technical has to be decided, people tend to accept the judgment of the person they believe knows more about

the matter than they do. Chances are, then, that workers in your unit look to you when difficult technical questions come up.

It is not necessary, of course, for a supervisor to have authority as the expert in every situation. If, for example, a complicated piece

An effective work team has group spirit and a sense of belonging, so that the whole is greater than the sum of its parts.

of equipment breaks down you might consult one of your workers who is an expert mechanic. You are likely to accept this worker's judgment about whether the machine should be repaired or replaced because you respect his or her superior knowledge.

It may surprise you to know that it is not enough to be a supervisor and to be expert in your line of work. It is not enough to have formal authority and the authority of the expert. If you are going to be an effective supervisor you must also have leadership authority.

If formal authority comes from management, we can say that leadership authority comes from the workers. Workers have to accept the fact that you are the supervisor. However, they do not have to accept you as their leader as well. You must *earn* their acceptance as their leader.

Workers select their own leader, who may or may not be the supervisor of their work unit. Once they have selected the leader they follow this person willingly, not because management has told them to do so. A supervisor who has not earned leadership authority will find that workers have assigned leadership to someone else. In many instances they will then follow the instructions of this leader rather than those of their supervisor. This can be a source of problems for the supervisor and for the local government in union and management relations where the employees are unionized.

It is difficult to get early warning signals of trouble from workers unless you have earned the position of leader. There is also no way of building a true work team if you have not earned the acceptance and respect of your workers as their leader.

Making jobs more interesting and rewarding

One of the more important skills a supervisor needs is the ability to redesign jobs so as to make them more interesting and challenging for workers. Many of us make the mistake of assuming that money and more money is what workers want most from their jobs. Yet time and again research has shown that this is simply not so.

A study in the early 1970s—one of the largest of its kind ever made—found that workers rank interesting work as the most important among twenty-five factors associated with work.

Over the past thirty years more than a hundred other studies have shown that workers also want to have more control over their work. Employees today—especially younger ones—rebel against work that is monotonous or meaningless. They want to feel that they are important and that the work they do is important. They resent being supervised too closely, or being pushed and threatened.

In short, employees want more authority to tackle their jobs on their own, more infor-

mation to enable them to do their work better, and greater opportunities for developing new skills or special abilities.

The time and effort a supervisor puts into enriching or redesigning his or her employees' jobs is likely to become visible in better employee attitude and morale, higher production, better work quality, lower turnover, and less absenteeism. Here are two examples of what job enrichment can accomplish.

Maintenance workers in one organization were not getting the buildings clean. In addition, the employee turnover rate was 100 percent every three months. In other words, four people had to be hired each year to keep one job filled!

Management learned from the workers that the problems were that the work was boring and that the workers had no say about how the work should be done. The solution was to enrich the workers' jobs by giving them more authority, more responsibility, and less supervision. Each worker was given a voice in planning work, setting goals, scheduling work, and figuring out how best to get the job done.

The result? The turnover rate dropped from 100 percent every three months to 10 percent. Building cleanliness increased by 20 percent. Sixty percent of the original workers were able to do the entire job, so that fewer workers had to be hired to replace those who left. And, finally, the organization saved $103,000 a year.

In another organization typists were copying form letters day after day in routine answers to letters received. These form letters were then proofed and signed by the supervisor. Turnover and absenteeism were high because the work was boring, offering neither challenge nor satisfaction. Management decided to allow typists to compose their own answers to the letters and also to proof and sign them. After this change was made, turnover was practically eliminated and absenteeism decreased by 30 percent.

One excellent way to make jobs more interesting is to *cross-train* your work team members. Let them learn how to do each other's jobs. As the supervisor, you can train them in the new skills that are required. Or, better yet, you can make the work of your team members even more interesting by having them cross-train each other. That way each has the chance to be a trainer as well as to learn a new skill. Cross-training also provides backup for your work team. If a team member is sick or absent, other team members can do that worker's job. One or another can fill in until the absent member returns to the team.

Coaching workers to improve their skills

In sports, a great team is often made up of players of average ability who become outstanding because of excellent coaching. Similarly, supervisors must coach workers of average ability to do above average work. If supervisors challenge their workers and help them gain the skills they need, most workers will surprise themselves with how well they can do the job.

Giving each employee an evaluation at the end of the year by filling out the required form is not very useful or constructive. This approach is like sitting in judgment on the worker—a report card rather than a joint learning process involving both the worker and the supervisor, or a way of developing the potential of the employee.

Good coaching requires that workers have positive, continuous feedback from supervisors. Positive feedback means that supervisors should praise both good work and improved work, in addition to helping correct mistakes. Instead of giving negative criticism, supervisors should show employees how to avoid and correct errors and how to learn from these errors.

Providing continuous feedback means giving workers frequent readings on how well they are doing individually and how well the team as a whole is progressing.

Checklist

Anticipate problems: try to identify problems which are just developing so that you can solve them early on.

Set clear goals for your work group: better yet, encourage your workers to help you set clear goals for the group. Try to ensure that organizational goals and employees' personal goals are combined and blended.

Build and maintain a work team.

Delegate work-related authority while retaining your supervisory authority.

Be a leader, not a boss.

Accept your responsibility as a supervisor for making jobs more interesting and challenging.

Be a developer of people, not a judge of employees.

LEADERSHIP

4

*When the best leader's work
is done the people say,
"We did it ourselves!"*

Lao-tzu

Chapter 4
LEADERSHIP

How does leadership differ from supervision?

How do effective leaders behave?

What skills do leaders possess?

How can a supervisor learn the art of leadership?

In the preceding chapter it was recommended that a supervisor try to become the leader of a team rather than merely being the person in charge of a group of workers. The point was also made that the authority a leader possesses comes from the workers themselves. When they become willing followers, the workers individually give their consent for a particular person to lead them. They might consent to follow the leadership of their supervisor—or they might select someone else. This person could be another member of the work group or someone who frequently relates to the membership of the group. When the workers follow the lead of someone other than their own supervisor, it could work against that supervisor's authority and effectiveness.

This chapter discusses the art of leadership, describing how effective leaders behave, what skills they possess, and what a supervisor needs to learn and practice to become a more effective leader.

What is leadership?

Management experts tend to disagree about leadership. Some believe a person is born with certain personality traits and abilities that make him or her a "natural" leader— the kind of individual that people admire, trust, and want to follow. Others believe that leadership depends on the situation. Such experts believe that while Franklin Roosevelt could lead the country out of a deep economic depression and successfully through most of a world war, he probably would not have been as effective on the battlefield. And while George Patton was an effective leader in battle, he probably would not have been as effective as the nation's president. Still other experts believe that both personality and situation are important factors in leadership.

Many managers wish that the experts could agree on what effective leadership is and which leadership style is "best." Unfortunately, leadership is not that simple. Because humans are so complex and so different from one another, even the experts have a hard time deciding what style of leadership works best in a particular situation.

The fact is that a supervisor may lead well under certain conditions and not so well under others. Factors beyond differences in the su-

pervisory situation itself can influence how effectively a supervisor is able to lead. One influencing factor is the maturity of the work group. Some work groups are more capable than others in setting challenging yet attainable goals. Some are more willing than others to assume responsibility for their own actions. In addition, work groups obviously vary in the level of member skill and experience.

Another influencing factor is the intensity of pressure or stress under which a work group is operating. In a situation involving high stress the work group may need and expect the leader to provide quick relief. Quite another leadership style may be the most appropriate when stress is not a critical element in the situation.

But while it may not be possible to outline one formula for how to be an effective leader in each and every supervisory situation, certain fundamentals about leadership are well established. A leader *leads*. A leader leads *willing* followers. And a leader leads in a *situation*—at work, on the battlefield, etc. Let us look at these elements as they relate to the supervisor's responsibilities.

Leader and followers

A leader can only lead by being "out in front" of the followers. This does not mean that a leader is always on the scene and is always more active personally than any of the followers. But a leader has a vision of what is needed, of what is possible, and of how to go about it.

A supervisor can be out in front of the followers in terms of ideas, as well as through the employment of proper supervisory practices, for example:

By seeing opportunities that others do not see

By identifying problems that are just developing and that the followers do not realize are taking form

---

By carrying out good planning so that there will be few, if any, crises or unpleasant surprises for the followers and many rewarding and unexpected accomplishments for them.

A leader is out in front of willing followers. The familiar saying "You can lead a horse to water, but you cannot make him drink" is an excellent illustration here. The important point is that the followers are willing. Tough, driving, self-serving, and inconsiderate bosses can get their subordinates to do work—but only up to a point. Workers may do what they are told to do when the boss is around, but when the boss is not around they will ease off. When, temporarily, they have had enough of their boss's pushing and driving, they may not come to work for a day or two.

And when, finally, they have had their fill of not being treated as human beings they often band together into a union. After that they will usually follow their union leader in challenging and opposing management actions that they consider unfair or improper.

A leader is able to gain and hold the loyalty of the workers so that they become willing followers. Loyalty is *earned* by a supervisor's actions. It cannot be demanded by a supervisor's rank or commanded by supervisory authority. It should be borne in mind that even when workers already are unionized a supervisor who is respected and trusted as a leader will be able to work effectively and cooperatively with the employees and their union representatives.

The supervisor who recognizes that each employee is a unique, distinctive individual with his or her own needs, personal likes and dislikes, strengths and weaknesses, and hopes and dreams has already taken the first large step toward earning the loyalty of those employees. And the supervisor who, out of a genuine interest in employees as individuals and through the use of correct supervisory practices, leads employees toward satisfaction of their needs and helps them to become what they can and want to become should be able to maintain leadership.

Situations and decisions

The situation surrounding each decision a supervisor must make is unique. Each situa-

tion has three elements that require sensitive consideration. These three elements are: (1) the nature of the problem requiring a supervisory decision, (2) the nature and mood of the employees in the work group at the time, and (3) the way the decision should be made.

The nature of the problem

When considering a problem that requires a decision, a supervisor should carefully examine three aspects of that problem that are directly related to gaining and maintaining leadership. The first aspect is the amount of information the supervisor possesses. Here you should ask yourself: Do I have the technical knowledge and all the facts required to make a sound decision, or do I need to obtain additional information or consult with others? If I need additional information, who has the knowledge or facts I require?

A second aspect concerns the efficient use of time. Here the question a supervisor should ask himself or herself is: How quickly do I need to act? In emergency situations where time is very important, you probably will want to decide quickly. But where time is not a critical factor, you may wish to make the decision using a different approach in order to gain long-term leadership benefits.

The third aspect to be examined is the importance of the decision to the supervisor's subordinates. You will want to ask yourself: Will the solution to the problem have im-

A leader: visualizes opportunities; identifies problems; plans for the situation; leads willing followers.

portant consequences for the members of the work group? If you believe it will, you should consult with your work team members before deciding.

Understanding the nature of the problem needing a supervisory decision is very important in making *correct* decisions. Poor understanding leads to wrong decisions; and supervisors who make many wrong decisions will have trouble convincing others to follow them.

The nature and mood of the employees

A second important element in the making of supervisory decisions is an understanding of and sensitivity to the work group and its individual members, especially an accurate "sensing" of the mood of the group at the time for decision. Understanding your employees is an ongoing supervisory process. It involves knowing their individual needs and abilities and keeping track of their skills development and the degree of teamwork shown. "Sensing" involves accurately gauging the group's current attitude, morale, level of motivation, and levels of fatigue and stress. If, for example, your team members are skilled and experienced, are functioning well as a team, have not been under any unusual pressures, and have trust in you and confidence in your decision making, involving them in every decision is unnecessary and can be inefficient. However, if your workers are not overly skilled or experienced, or have not

been functioning as a team, or have been under some pressure recently, or perhaps do not trust management entirely, involving them in decision making to a substantial degree might be a desirable way of improving relations and increasing productivity.

The way the decision should be made

When you have considered the nature of the problem and have carefully "read" the mood and current organizational needs of your workers and of the work group, you are in a position to choose the way you should proceed:

The *tell/sell/test/consult/join* model is a very helpful tool for a supervisor at this point. If you, the supervisor, have the necessary skill and information to make the decision and your "sensing" of the mood of your work team suggests this is a proper way to decide, then *tell* your group what should be done and perhaps even how it should be done as well. This is an efficient way to use your supervisory time. It is also an especially appropriate way to make decisions in emergency situations or when your workers are operating under high stress.

If you have the necessary skill and information to make the required decision yourself but believe that your work group members might not understand your decision and might not fully support it, then you may need

to *sell* your decision to your work team. Explain why you decided as you did, and strive to convince them that it was the proper decision to make under the circumstances. When they understand all the facts, they probably will support your decision. Sometimes you may want to sell to your work team a decision you plan to make, so that the members will understand your decision and support it when it is made.

If you feel the need to *test* some or all of your alternatives before making a decision, you may wish to use some members or all of your work team as a sounding board to get suggestions and reactions to the choices you are considering. You may actually undertake a trial run of a new way of doing the job or a new technique to see how well it works.

When you don't have all the technical knowledge or facts necessary to make a correct decision, then you will want to *consult* with some or all members of your work team or with your superior or others who have the knowledge or information you need and who can advise you as to the best way to proceed.

And there are many, many situations in which the best way to decide is to *join* with your work team members, allowing them to participate fully with you in making the decision.

Knowing when to decide by yourself and when and to what degree to share decision making

Employees should not be involved in every supervisory decision.

with your employees is very important in the earning and holding of leadership. A good rule to follow is: if the decision is going to affect the workers directly—for example, by adding to the work they do, by changing the work they do or the way they do it, by making them feel less secure, by requiring them to "stretch" their skills and abilities, by affecting their pay or benefits or free time—then involve them in the decision-making process if you possibly can. Giving the workers a voice in deciding those things that affect them directly and personally will help win their willingness to cooperate with you in the decision that is made. It is important not only to make correct decisions, but also to make them in the proper way.

Characteristics of leader–supervisors

Supervisors who are truly leaders differ from other supervisors in four important ways. First, supervisors who are leaders have a personal and active attitude toward goals. They have a strong vision of what could be and should be and are able to pass this on to others. Supervisors who are not leaders tend to have a passive attitude toward goals. They may see goals as necessary because the organization requires goals. They do not see them as a means toward a *desired* end.

Second, leaders are willing to take some risks—carefully considered risks—in order to reach a desired end. Ordinary supervisors tend to do things "by the book."

Third, leaders inspire others and enable others to identify with them, to become "committed to the cause," whereas ordinary supervisors merely *work with* people in a decision-making process.

Fourth, leaders try to change or improve those things that need to be changed or improved, while ordinary supervisors see themselves as regulators of the status quo.

Leadership attitudes

The style of leadership that a supervisor uses is the product of that supervisor's attitudes and assumptions about people, about their competence, and about how to get work done. Some supervisors believe that being interested in getting work done and being interested in people are contradictory concepts.

Therefore, some supervisors focus their attention and effort on production alone. These supervisors tend to view workers as mere tools for getting the job done. They tend to believe that if they had "better" people they could get more and better work done. They are the tough, driving "bosses."

Then there are other supervisors (and these also believe that concern with work and concern with people are in conflict) who assume that *all* people are dedicated and hardworking and that the supervisor's task is to take care of employees and to try to keep them happy. They focus their supervisory attention and effort on creating and maintaining a "happy family" relationship among their subordinates. This type is the "sweetheart" supervisor.

Still other supervisors (who also believe concern for work and concern for people are contradictory) personally have a low level of motivation, or do not think of themselves as supervisors at all, but rather as more experienced police officers, or firefighters, or accountants, perhaps. This type tends not to focus attention and effort on either production or people. This person is the "indifferent" supervisor.

Still other supervisors, while believing that concern for work and concern for people are in conflict, try to balance out the two. They try to find a compromise between the organization's needs and those of the workers. These "balancer" supervisors may attempt to spend half their time on work and the other half on people. Some supervisors of this type manage "by crisis." They focus on production when the work is behind schedule or when there are no obvious serious problems involving people. But as soon as they believe that significant problems are developing with people, they tend to forget about work responsibilities and to concentrate on people. While they are doing this the work may again fall behind, thereby producing another crisis.

The effective *leader–supervisor* does not see a conflict between work and people. He or she does not believe that workers are lazy

Your leadership style says a great deal about your perceptions of people.

and must therefore be pushed and driven. Nor does this type of supervisor believe that everyone will work hard if the supervisor leaves them alone, or makes them happy. Effective leader–supervisors think that it is possible to blend concern for work and concern for people. They feel that if work is made more interesting and meaningful, and if workers can satisfy their own personal needs through work, then a lot of high-quality work will be done because the workers *want* to do it and gain satisfaction from doing it.

Leadership behaviors

A supervisor's set of attitudes and assumptions about people and how best to get work done influences how that supervisor will behave when planning or attempting to get work done. These same attitudes and assumptions will probably influence the way in which a supervisor evaluates how well a job is done or how well a worker is performing.

Planning the work

Tough, driving "bosses" do the planning themselves and typically do not involve their subordinates. They tend to use personal standards in making planning decisions, such as, "That's the way *I* want it," or, "You'll do it that way because that's the way *I* like it done."

"Sweetheart" supervisors usually do not plan unless the work group wants to, and then only because it will make the workers happy.

"Indifferent" supervisors tend to use "how we've always done it" or the organization manual as the basis of planning. In that way they avoid investing much of themselves in this supervisory function.

"Balancer" supervisors tend to do the planning themselves until it is *time* to be concerned with people. Then they may share the planning with their subordinates.

Effective leader–supervisors strive to involve their team members in planning—especially in those areas where the members' personal interests and concerns are strong. They encourage participation, to gain a higher level of commitment from the team members and because they truly believe that "many heads are better than one."

Getting the work done

As with the planning function, a supervisor's attitudes and assumptions about the nature and competence of people influence how that supervisor will behave in attempting to get tasks accomplished.

Tough, driving "bosses," since they believe that workers are lazy and are attempting to avoid work, will try to be at the work scene as much as possible, personally providing step-by-step direction to the workers. The underlying supervisory attitude here is perhaps best expressed in the following two statements: "As soon as you turn your head, they'll goof off on you," and, "If you're not right on

top of things every minute, they'll goof up and do it all wrong."

"Sweetheart" supervisors frequently provide no direction to the workers. They concern themselves more with supporting their workers—providing satisfaction for their morale needs and answering their technical questions. A "sweetheart" supervisor might be concerned primarily with making sure a street-paving crew has cold drinking water at the work site or with breaking off work early if the day has been exceptionally hot.

The "indifferent" supervisor tends to tell the workers what needs to be done and how, and then to avoid further contact with the work and workers unless a problem arises.

"Balancer" supervisors tend to tell the workers what needs to be done and how. They usually then advise them that if any problems develop they should let the supervisor know immediately. If work is running behind schedule such a supervisor may spend more time on the scene and may behave more like the tough, driving "boss." When things are going well again this supervisor may spend some time "mending fences" with workers.

The effective leader–supervisor tries to function as a member of the team while the work is being done. He or she does this not by doing work along with the others but rather by providing such special skills and knowledge as he or she may have and by promoting teamwork.

One skill quite useful to the leader–supervisor in getting more work done willingly and well is the *art of delegation*. Less effective supervisors either do not delegate at all or go to the other extreme and give up their supervisory authority, allowing the workers to take charge. The supervisor who does not or cannot delegate ends up trying to do everything personally—planning, deciding how things should be done, directing and controlling employees as they do the work, checking up on the quality of performance, and so on. There are, after all, only so many hours in a day. And a supervisor cannot be in more than one place at a time. Furthermore, we all have limits as to how far we can push ourselves. Therefore, the supervisor who does not delegate places severe limits on how much can be done. And the supervisor who cannot tell the difference between delegation and abandonment of supervisory authority will lose control of the situation and the work group.

True delegation by a supervisor involves giving the "how to do it" authority to those members of the work team who have the necessary job skills and experience and whose attitude toward the organization is positive. If a member does not have sufficient skill or experience to be entrusted with the authority to decide how   that is, by what methods—the work should be done, then the supervisor needs to work with that person to increase his or her skills and experience. And when there is a team member whose attitude

may be less than that desired, the supervisor should relate to and work with that employee to help him or her develop a more positive attitude.

What a supervisor *should not* delegate is the authority he or she has in relation to the whole team. And, of course, a supervisor *can never delegate* the responsibility for the team that has been assigned by superiors and the accountability to those superiors for the team's attitude, morale, work behavior, and performance.

A helpful rule to follow with regard to proper delegation is: "Keep your hands *on* the work situation, not *in* it."

Evaluating individual and group effort and performance

Again, what a supervisor believes about employees and how best to handle work and people will influence how that supervisor will evaluate performance.

Tough, driving "bosses" tend to fix their attention on mistakes. They look for things that are wrong, often overlooking those things that are done well. When they find a mistake they criticize the person who made it. Often they suggest a penalty that will be forthcoming if the mistake is repeated. Some genuinely believe they are developing competence and maturity in their subordinates, although their usual attitude is: "The tool is

not working properly; therefore, fix it so that it won't break down again." This type of supervisor usually provides only negative feedback to the workers.

"Sweetheart" supervisors tend to say nothing if they cannot pay a compliment. They have the following attitude: "We're all human and make mistakes, so let's forget it and get on with the work." This style of supervisor tends to provide only positive feedback to employees.

"Indifferent" supervisors usually provide no feedback at all unless they are required to do so by the organization. Then, typically, they merely fill out the required performance evaluation form. Usually, when filling out such a form, they score their subordinates in the middle of the range. They feel that in this way they will not get in trouble with their superiors by scoring too high or with their workers by scoring too low.

"Balancer" supervisors focus on both successes and mistakes, trying to offset a criticism with a compliment. Preceding criticism with a compliment, however, causes a worker to question the sincerity of the compliment. Frequently, such supervisors practice the technique of criticizing in private and complimenting in the group setting.

Effective leader–supervisors provide feedback continually. When things are going well the supervisor and the team members together discuss how and why this is so. When things are not going well they discuss how to set them right. When an individual is not doing things properly, the supervisor and the employee get together to plan what needs to be done to correct matters. The leader–supervisor wants to develop people as a means of improving the work. This type of approach enables the supervisor to increase the skills and abilities of the team members and to develop the capabilities of the team as a whole.

Together, the attitudes and assumptions about people and the behaviors a supervisor demonstrates on the job add up to a supervisor's leadership style.

The most successful and respected supervisors follow rules that say, in effect, "Treat people like adults," "Respect your subordinates as the unique individuals they are," "Develop your team members into truly outstanding individuals and workers," "Coach your people into becoming a winning team and winners as individuals." Remember that the key elements in achieving excellence in a work team are *trusting*, *respecting*, *developing*, and *coaching*.

And if you, the supervisor, behave like a highly effective leader–supervisor, you:

Show that you value your people just as highly as you value your production goals

Are honest in your relations with people

Are open and truly listen

Encourage input and participation

Are sensitive to the needs and feelings of your team members.

If you do these things, then the work team will have pride, will be highly productive, and will do excellent work.

Checklist

To check on your leadership, try to judge whether your subordinates would "elect" you as their supervisor if they had the chance. If you think they might not, ask yourself why.

Draw up a mental picture of what you would like your work group to do and become in the future.

Ask yourself: "Do my workers frequently volunteer to do things? Do they do what needs to be done without being told, or do they usually have to be told what to do?" If they usually must be told, ask yourself why.

Try to avoid always using the same decision-making approach—for example, making most of the decisions yourself. Let the situation determine which approach is best.

Ask yourself whether you have a fairly accurate understanding of your workers' needs, desires, and concerns, and a fairly accurate sense of your work group's current mood and why it is such.

Ask yourself what assumptions you tend to make about your workers. Are they correct assumptions?

Think carefully about your relations with your employees, and then ask yourself: "Am I a 'boss,' a 'sweetheart,' an 'indifferent' supervisor, a 'balancer'? Do I manage 'by crisis,' or am I truly a leader–supervisor?"

Learn how leader–supervisors typically plan, work with team members to get work done, and evaluate how work is going, and then try to practice these approaches and techniques.

Keep your hands on the work and the work situation, but avoid getting into everything.

COMMUNICATING
WITH
EMPLOYEES

The very word "communicate" means "share"

Colin Cherry

Chapter 5
COMMUNICATING WITH EMPLOYEES

How do you communicate effectively?

What is the communication process?

What are barriers to effective communication?

What are formal and informal channels of communication?

How can you be a better listener?

"Those guys never do what's expected of them."

"It seems that Susan can't follow my simplest instructions."

"I can't figure out where they got an idea like that!"

"How was I to know Ray was upset? He said he was okay."

"Why didn't someone tell me there was a problem?"

More often than we realize, the observation of the warden in the movie *Cool Hand Luke* rings true: "What we have here is a failure to communicate." We are frustrated and surprised when people misinterpret or do not understand what we say. Because we have been expressing ourselves all our lives, we assume that we communicate well, almost as easily and naturally as we breathe. The truth is that although we may be talking, we may not be communicating effectively. Effective communication usually demands a great deal of effort, practice, and understanding.

If the supervisor's job is "to get work done through others," then communication is a necessary part of supervision. In fact, supervisory relationships could not exist without effective communication. Whenever workers join together to accomplish given tasks, they must communicate. To direct the combined efforts of a work group, a supervisor must somehow tell employees about plans, ideas, and directions so that they can carry them out. Most supervisors probably spend more than half their time communicating in some way—training employees, giving work assignments, demonstrating procedures or equipment, conducting staff meetings, answering questions, listening to employee concerns, helping citizens with problems, and discussing plans and operations with managers and other supervisors.

Supervisors communicate in many different ways. They may talk face to face to groups or individual employees; they may use a telephone or a two-way radio; they may write letters, memos, or bulletins. They may also communicate through gestures or signals, facial expressions, or silence. Regardless of the extent or method, without effective communication, supervisors and workers may find themselves working at cross purposes, pursuing competing objectives, duplicating one another's efforts, and failing to complete necessary jobs.

What is communication?

One definition of communication is "behavior that transmits meaning from one person to another." This definition seems simple enough, but actually it is very complex. Let's look closely at its individual parts.

"Behavior that transmits meaning . . ." can be more than words—much more. Facial expressions, posture, tone of voice, and even silence tell a person about the feelings, thoughts, and attitudes of another person. Through one of many methods, we can transfer, share, or convey a "*meaning from one person to another.*" The definition says that any transmission that exchanges meaning is communication, but it does not say whether the meaning is clear or unclear.

Communication is a process because it involves activity. We must do something in order to exchange feelings, facts, ideas, and meaning. Something must happen between two or more people. But what exactly happens?

To answer this question, let's look at the elements of the communication process. These are the *sender*, the *message*, the *medium*, the *receiver*, the *feedback*, and the *environment*.

When we transmit feelings, facts, or ideas to others, we become *senders*. The sender initiates the transfer of meaning. A sender appearing before a group of people may be referred to as the talker, speaker, or presenter. During one-on-one conversations, both the parties alternate as senders.

The *message* is the feeling, fact, or idea the sender conveys to the receiver. Because we cannot directly exchange with someone else what we are experiencing, we translate the experience into symbols. Symbols such as words and gestures permit us to describe, explain, and share with others what we feel, know, or think so that it has meaning to them.

The *medium* is the means the sender uses to transmit the message. Although the most commonly used means are speaking and writing, physical touch and body movement also serve as ways to transfer a message from one person to another. Often the sender uses more than one medium at the same time and sends the message through more than one of the receiver's five senses. In fact, using two or more senses may enhance the communication process (seeing and hearing, plus touch—a handshake—for instance).

The person who gets the message is called the *receiver*. A group of receivers may be called the audience or the listeners. In one-

Working together depends on communication.

on-one conversations, both parties become receivers. In seeing, hearing, or feeling, receivers create a frame of reference and change messages into experiences with meaning for themselves.

As the receiver attempts to understand the message, he or she usually reacts in some manner. This reaction is called *feedback*. Nodding the head, for instance, may signal agreement or understanding while shaking the head may indicate disagreement or frustration. Facial expressions and body movements may show pleasure, discomfort, boredom, or confusion. Feedback tells the sender how well the message is being received.

The *environment* is both the physical location and the conditions existing when communication occurs. Noise, lighting, and time of day may improve or hinder communication. In fact, the environment itself—colors, seating arrangements, lighting—may communicate a great deal to the receiver. It is very important for the sender to consider the impact a particular setting or certain conditions can have on communication.

Effective communication

We see, then, that communication is actually a process involving a number of steps. Using this process, a person can communicate meaning to another person. However, what the sender means and what the receiver "hears" or understands may be very different. Even if we do a very good job of sending our message, how do we know that others receive it correctly? Our communication efforts may not always be very effective!

Let's carry our discussion a little further. Effective communication is behavior that transmits a meaning (message) from one person (sender) to another (receiver) so that it is mutually understood. By *mutually understood*, we mean the receiver understands the same message the sender understands.

Many breakdowns in communication occur when the sender gives a message one meaning and the receiver gives it another. Misreading "simple" instructions in assembling a child's toy or getting lost following "you-can't-miss-it" directions are examples of communication breakdowns.

A shared understanding of the message is critical for effective communication. Expressing feelings, facts, or ideas to our own satisfaction is not enough because what seems clear to us may not be clear to someone else. We must say what we mean so that others will understand us.

Feedback is a crucial part of effective communication. It enables the sender to know what message the receiver understands. Feedback enables the sender to change, adapt, revise, or clarify communication to the receiver, thereby improving the likelihood that the receiver will understand the meaning intended.

Symbols

We communicate meaning to one another through symbols representing a message. A supervisor who wants to communicate with an employee in order to discipline, explain, praise, or recognize that person may do so verbally or nonverbally. Verbal communication is the most obvious kind of symbolic communication. Most supervisors would say they usually communicate verbally with employees. However, much of the communication between supervisors and employees does not involve words. Because of the subtle ways that we continually communicate nonverbally, it may be impossible not to communicate when we are with others. Let's examine some of those ways.

Paralanguage, or voice characteristics, is closely related to verbal communication, but it concerns *how* something is said, rather than *what* is said. It involves the tone of voice, pitch, emphasis, speed, loudness, and pauses we use in speaking. The same words may communicate various meanings depending on how these words are expressed. For example, a supervisor who says, "I am not upset with your work," may give the statement many different meanings by saying it many different ways.

Often, how something is said is just as important as what is said in communication between supervisors and employees. Paralanguage can communicate meanings in ways that words alone cannot.

Body language, another type of nonverbal communication, involves the position or movement of the body—posture, gestures, and facial expressions. Unintentionally, a supervisor may communicate much to an employee through body language. A clenched fist may signal anger, worry, or tension. Eye contact may communicate honesty, attention, or interest. Playing with a pencil, tapping fingers on a desk, or gazing out the window when an employee is talking may communicate lack of interest or boredom.

Physical space around and between people also communicates meaning. Informal space is the physical distance revealing emotional distance between people. We permit those close to us emotionally to be close to us physically, and we tend to be uncomfortable when crowded into an elevator or seated next to strangers.

How you say something is just as important as what you say.

If we move too close when approaching someone, that person may back away. If we stop too far away, the other person may come closer. We each have our own idea of personal space and we expect most types of communication to take place at a "normal" distance. A supervisor standing "in an employee's face" may be threatening that person. In the same way, a supervisor who stands so that touching the employee "with a ten-foot pole" is impossible may be communicating dislike or disapproval.

The furniture arrangement in an office is an example of semi-fixed space as a means of communication. If a supervisor sits behind a desk and employees sit in front, the desk becomes a barrier representing formality, superiority, or authority. If the supervisor moves to a chair next to the employee, the desk barrier is removed and both parties are on an equal basis. The employee may relax somewhat because the situation seems friendly and informal.

Nonverbal communication, with symbols, is exchanged in a variety of other ways. Some years ago, the Broadway production *Hair* dealt in part with the 1960s conflict over hair length. Like parents and kids, supervisors and employees have fought and argued about hair length. As the play indicated, the real issue is not hair, but what it communicates and symbolizes.

Much of what we communicate is based on such symbols, in our personal lives as well

You communicate by your appearance and facial expression as well as by what you say.

as in work situations. The symbols of our jobs—the vehicles we drive, the clothes we wear, the equipment we use, the way we carry out our duties—communicate a great deal about us and our work for local government to citizens and other employees.

The supervisor, therefore, must consider nonverbal as well as verbal communication. The supervisor should be aware that such things as intonation, inflection, actions, setting, behavior, informal space, and personal appearance can communicate meaning.

Channels of communication

The expression "you have to go through the proper channels" applies to communication because messages are translated through channels into symbols others can receive. Channels are the medium for transferring messages from the supervisor to others in the organization.

Oral channels include face-to-face communication as well as the loudspeaker, telephone, radio, and other electronic media. Written channels include letters, memos, bulletins, manuals, handbooks, brochures, and pamphlets.

The channel we choose is important: communicating with someone face to face is different from telephoning or writing a letter, even when the same words are used. Receiving a memo from the boss is obviously

different from being called to the boss's office about the same issue.

Face-to-face communication usually conveys nonverbal symbols such as body language, as well as verbal symbols. The receiver can hear the speaker's tone of voice and emphasis on certain words and can give immediate feedback through facial expressions, gestures, or words. Telephoning also has the advantage of producing immediate (verbal) feedback.

Written communication, however, depends almost entirely on understanding of printed words. Feedback for written communication is limited. For example, someone reading this page is less likely to give the author feedback (by writing a letter or telephoning) than a person listening to the author speak in a classroom.

In every local government or organization, there are two different, important kinds of communication channels: the formal or official channels and the informal channels known sometimes as the "grapevine." Formal channels are established to permit information to flow through the organization. Typically following existing lines of authority in the organization, formal channels take three forms and serve three primary purposes.

Downward communication directs the work effort. Goals and objectives designed at the top level of the organization are passed down

to managers, supervisors, and finally to workers. This process links the various levels together in pursuit of the organization's mission. Policies, orders, procedures, and assignments are carried out through downward communication.

Upward communication keeps those at higher levels informed about the work effort. Essentially, it yields feedback about what is taking place at the various levels of the organization. Supervisors play a critical role in upward and downward communication because they link management and employees.

Horizontal communication takes place between people on the same level but in different areas or departments. Its primary purpose is to coordinate effort and work assignments. To avoid downtime or duplication, to improve the efficiency and effectiveness of local government service delivery, supervisors use horizontal communication.

Informal channels exist outside the organization's formal channels, but they play an important role in communicating information within the organization. The continual interaction of employees at all levels—supervisors and subordinates, co-workers, peers in different departments—is a vital part of the total communication process that makes local government organizations function effectively. Informal communication tends to be quick and believable—that is, information moves quickly through informal channels and is often more readily accepted than official messages. The informal channels may become busier when formal channels don't provide enough information or don't provide it when it is expected or needed. Sometimes it is easier for management to be heard and understood if the message is shared informally rather than sent through the formal system. An effective manager knows that many important messages—some of them accurate, official, or sanctioned, some not— flow through the informal system.

Generally, a manager or supervisor has more control and influence over the formal channels of communication than over the informal system. One person or a few people decide what information goes into the formal system, when, and in what format. But a message that will travel unchanged through the formal channels may be reworked, filtered, or distorted as it works its way through the informal system. Therefore it is important for you to be receptive to both channels regardless of your position in the organization.

Barriers to effective communication

One metaphor depicts communication as a conveyor belt moving packages: a bundle transported along a conveyor belt from point A to point B arrives as the same package, unchanged. Unfortunately, communication does not work this way. The message we package in symbols and send to our receiver may become something entirely different when the receiver opens or interprets the package.

We have all used expressions such as "I don't see things your way" or "I see the situation somewhat differently from you." What we mean is that our perception is different. We know, for instance, that if ten different people witness an accident, each one will have a slightly different impression of what happened. And if participants in a training class are asked to look out a window and to describe in a paragraph what they see, each one will describe the same scene in a different way.

Perception is the way we "see" things. It is based on environment, experience, and motivation. No two people will have the same perception because perception is as unique and individual as are the employees in a work group. Each worker grows up in a different family, experiences different events in life, and has individual needs and goals. For this reason, employees will have various perceptions of their supervisor, their work, and their co-workers.

No two people hear things the same way.

For example, an employee reared in a permissive family environment may resent the rules and orders of a supervisor with years of military experience who thinks "standard operating procedure" is important. On the other hand, a worker strongly committed to authority and "chain-of-command" principles may perceive a supervisor seeking input and participation as wishy-washy, uncertain, or unknowledgeable.

Prejudice—pre-judging—is an example of the possible negative impact of perception. It may cause us to see and hear only what we want to see and hear, producing false ideas about others and what they want to communicate. Even before a black or female or a "long-haired" worker speaks, some supervisors have already determined the value of what this worker will say.

Problems in perception may be the primary reason communication between people sometimes breaks down. We use common symbols as a means for communicating, but these symbols are still subject to individual interpretation. And our interpretation depends on our perception of ourselves, others, and the world around us.

Many other barriers to effective communication exist, some of which are closely related to perception. Useful as they are, words still create a variety of problems. As mentioned earlier, words are merely symbols with attached meanings. And while we have a general or common understanding about the meaning of most words, the meaning is often vague or imprecise. What a word means to one person may not be exactly what it means to someone else. The meaning of words may change with time or between cultural groups.

Words such as "tight," "bad," "cool," "space," and "tough" have different meanings for today's young people than for those of other generations. New words like "microchip," "data processing," and "software" weren't even used by earlier generations. Words such as "environment," "ecology," and "system" have become increasingly popular, while others like "phonograph," "outhouse," and "buggy" are no longer common.

Words can mean different things to different people even though those people are the same age and have had similar experiences. For example, let's say a supervisor tells Jane to "run over" to the supply room for a spare part. Does this mean that Jane is to run or just walk briskly? And if the supervisor says "hurry," should Jane go as quickly as possible, throwing caution to the wind, or only as fast as safety permits? Is it okay for her to stop and speak to someone else "for just a second" while hurrying?

Suppose that a supervisor evaluating Jim's performance says that a poor work attitude is obvious—what is obvious to Jim? That Jim's performance is poor? That, though Jim's performance is good, he seems unhappy? Or that Jim seems not to like the supervisor, or vice versa?

The difficulty with words, then, is that because we give them individual meanings or use them differently, what we communicate often depends on the other person's interpretation. This situation is similar to the game "Password," in which people take turns trying to understand messages from each other.

Another barrier to effective communication is noise. Noise, in terms of communication, is defined as a distraction or interference that disrupts the transfer of messages between people. Obviously, carrying on a conversation is difficult in a busy office where people are typing and phones are ringing, or at a worksite where machinery is operating or traffic is moving. The noise may be so loud that we cannot "hear ourselves think," much less communicate with someone else. Physical noise prevents us from receiving.

However, noise can be internal as well as external. Internal noises include personal problems, conflicts, daydreams—whatever occupies a person's mind when you are attempting to communicate with that person. Instead of hearing what you have to say, the person is, in a very real sense, hearing something else.

For example, a supervisor may want to remind Bob of something that needs to be done "first thing Monday morning." The supervisor mentions this to Bob just before the workday ends on Friday. Bob, however, is already thinking about a weekend trip and consciously or unconsciously tunes out his

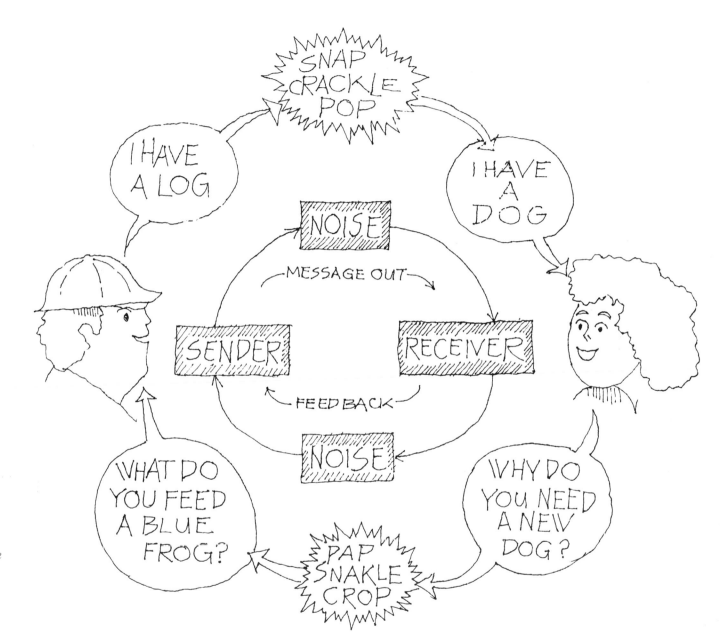

Noise disturts the message
from sender . . .
to receiver . . .
to sender.

supervisor. Bob "hears" but he just doesn't listen. Conversely, suppose Bob tries to discuss a problem with his supervisor. The supervisor at that moment is more concerned with an upcoming purchase order or a meeting with the department head, and listening to Bob is difficult for the supervisor.

Noise, both internal and external, may cause numerous messages to be missed or misunderstood. Good communicators try to eliminate such distractions by choosing a time and place that will enhance listening and thus be conducive to effective communication.

Finally, a sender can create another barrier by using a one-way communication channel. It is typical for us to place the responsibility for listening on the receiver of a message. In fact, the receiver is commonly referred to as the listener, while the sender is called the speaker. This is accurate, however, only if we view communication as a one-way process.

If a person assumes that the sender's job is to express the message and the receiver's job is to hear it, that person ignores the role that feedback plays in communication. This would be equivalent to ignoring someone who asks a question. If a sender uses one-way communication only, the opportunity is missed to provide further information, to clarify a point, or to correct an error.

Unfortunately, this situation is exactly what sometimes unfolds when supervisors and employees try to communicate. Some supervisors miss feedback—facial expressions, tone of voice, oral statements and questions, or plain silence—simply because they are too busy communicating on a one-way channel.

Improving communication skills

Communication is easy; effective communication is not. As we have said, it is simple for us to express ourselves—through spoken and written language, gestures, facial expressions, and a host of other symbols. But *effective* communication is much more difficult.

Improving communication skills is of particular importance to supervisors because communication is so closely related to supervisory effectiveness. A good supervisor is also a good communicator. Through feedback, active listening, and the use of formal channels, a supervisor can improve communication.

Feedback

No matter how well supervisors and employees express themselves (or think they do), many barriers to communication can still exist. Obtaining feedback is the best way to overcome the barriers because it lets us check what we said or heard. The supervisor, as a good communicator, must both *give* and *receive* feedback.

Supervisors should give employees feedback to tell them how they are doing. Feedback can be used to discipline, correct, inform, or praise the performance of employees. Often employees really do not know whether they are doing good work or poor work. Why? Because they are not receiving feedback about their jobs.

Many supervisors mistakenly assume that employees know both how well they are doing and how well their supervisors think they are doing. It is the supervisor's responsibility to tell employees about their performance through feedback.

Giving feedback to all employees—good and poor—is important. If we offer feedback just to poor performers, we ignore the needs of good employees who should be recognized for their efforts. It is human nature to want praise for a job well done. And giving positive feedback is worth the supervisor's time.

Although it is not easy to offer negative comments, constructive criticism is important for less productive workers who may think you are satisfied with their work. By not disciplining or correcting them through feedback, you may be implying that you are pleased with their poor performance.

An evaluation once or twice a year should not be the only time when a supervisor gives employees feedback. Remarks should be offered at appropriate times and locations. For example, do not give an employee negative feedback in front of co-workers—your primary purpose is to help, not to embarrass, your employees. Whether positive or negative, feedback can and should be used to help employees know where they stand and adjust their performances accordingly.

It is just as important that supervisors receive feedback. Have you ever ended a work-day wondering whether your employees think you are doing a good job? Or agonized over a tough personnel decision and then tried to guess whether the jury (your employees) judged you innocent or guilty? Have you disciplined a worker and then tried to imagine how that person felt? Or have you ever conducted a training session on new equipment or procedures and wondered whether your employees really understood what you explained? Supervisors who receive feedback from their employees are more likely to have answers to these and similar questions.

Receiving feedback is sometimes difficult for supervisors because of the barrier created by their positions. Supervisors who are good communicators can overcome this problem to some degree. They encourage feedback by being receptive and open to their workers' complaints and concerns. These supervisors also do another very important thing: they solicit feedback.

The feedback a supervisor receives, however, largely depends on how he or she re-

quests it. For example, suppose a supervisor explains a new work method to an employee and then asks, "Do you understand?" We know the answer is likely to be "yes." If the supervisor asks instead, "What do you understand?" the feedback will be much more informative.

It is important for supervisors to realize that when they ask for feedback they might just get it! And although all feedback from employees may not be positive, all of it can be helpful. The kind of feedback your employees give you will be influenced by how willing you seem to accept it.

In both giving and receiving feedback, supervisors should deal with feelings as well as thoughts. Supervisors must be willing to express their feelings to employees and to give employees a chance to share their reactions and feelings. Feelings are real. Supervisors and employees will find that dealing openly with feelings is the best practice.

Listening

Being a good listener is the best way for supervisors to encourage feedback. Listening is another ability of supervisors who are good communicators.

To improve our communication skills, we have to become active listeners. Too many of us think listening is a passive, easy activity de-

manding little from us. Active listening is hard work. It requires us to give our undivided attention to another person and to attempt to understand what is being communicated. As a supervisor, you can communicate that you are actively listening in several ways.

Face the worker and look at him or her attentively. If your gaze moves to the clock or around the room, the worker may interpret these actions as displaying a lack of interest.

Show that you are following the conversation by making facial expressions, by nodding occasionally, or by saying, "I see."

Wait patiently if the worker talks slowly or becomes silent—this gives the person time to collect thoughts and to consider what has been said.

Avoid interrupting the worker by talking, finishing sentences for him or her, or answering calls.

Listen not only to what the person is saying but also to the feelings being expressed.

When workers come to you to discuss difficulties, they are telling you more than just facts. They are telling you not only what happened but also how they feel about it and they are doing so through verbal and non-verbal means. You should notice facial expressions, body stance, tone of voice, position, and hand movements.

Many people are uncomfortable when talking about feelings—yours as well as their own. They may think that being angry, jealous, or depressed is wrong, and they may find it difficult to admit these feelings even to themselves. However, ignoring feelings is overlooking information needed to solve problems.

To "listen" for feelings, you should pay attention not only to what the worker is saying but also to how he or she is saying it. If John says he feels fine, but he has a worried look on his face and a strained voice, you may guess that something is bothering him. If Mary insists she is not upset, but her face is red, her fists are clenched, and her gaze is unsteady, you may guess that she is not being completely honest.

Active listening helps supervisors "hear" more than the words of their employees. Feedback becomes an integral part of the active listening process. It lets your workers know you are truly listening. Sometimes it is helpful to paraphase the worker's message by beginning with a statement such as "What you're saying is..." or "Sounds like you're feeling...." By listening attentively, supervisors may come to appreciate their workers'

concerns and may be able to help resolve them. Consider the following situation.

Harry, a worker, says to his supervisor, "This job really depresses me. I no sooner finish one thing than they bring me something else to do. Sometimes I think they think I'm a machine."

A supervisor who considers only Harry's words might immediately try to devise a way for Harry to do his job faster or might get someone to help Harry do his work. A supervisor who is listening to the feelings in Harry's message may suspect that Harry is complaining about more than just the workload. Harry may be saying indirectly that his only reward for doing his work is receiving more work. He may be frustrated because his supervisor has not recognized his efforts with a word of praise or appreciation.

A supervisor who wants to discover what sparked Harry's comment will check out an array of possible reasons, perhaps saying, "You know, Harry, we *have* been very busy lately. I can see how it would be frustrating to you and I haven't even been by here lately to let you know how much I appreciate the fine job you're doing."

This kind of response opens the door for the worker to share what is really on his or her mind and gives you a chance to listen. The supervisor, then, has an opportunity to learn if the employee feels that the workload is

really too great or that the amount of received praise is too small, or a combination of both. That you can learn more by listening than by talking may be true—supervisors would do well to practice their listening skills.

Supervisors must also improve their skills of expression. There is no need to impress employees with your command of the English language or your technical expertise. It is important that your employees realize that *you* know what you are talking about, but it may be even more important that *they* understand what you are saying.

Your workers will undoubtedly have various educational backgrounds and work experiences. Supervisors who are good communicators try to take these differences into account when communicating with their workers. Some workers may understand an explanation that only confuses others.

As a supervisor, you will spend a good part of your time trying to make sure that all your workers understand what you are saying. The following considerations may help you in your efforts at effective communication.

Keep in mind that each worker is different and that what succeeds with one may fail with another.

Use simple and direct language. Just because something is easy for some to understand does not mean everyone can understand it.

Repeat what is important for your workers to understand. Remember that much of what we learn is based on repetition.

Communicate the same message in different ways. For example, in training employees, you may use discussions, written materials, demonstrations, and visual aids to communicate your message.

Use open-ended questions. Open-ended questions, those which cannot be responded to with a simple "yes" or "no," tell us whether employees are understanding us.

Remember that face-to-face communication works best because it provides an opportunity for direct, immediate interaction between supervisors and employees.

Formal channels

Supervisors who are good communicators use the formal channels of communication in their local government. Their participation is critical for facilitating effective communication between employees and management.

Supervisors should use downward communication to keep their employees informed.

Workers want to know about decisions being made that directly affect them. They want to know what changes they can anticipate. Such information should always be presented to workers in a positive and constructive way. The supervisor has a duty to support directives from above and to communicate his or her support to workers. If you tell your workers, "I don't like these changes, but . . .," or "I can't agree with their decision, but . . .," or "I know this isn't going to work because . . .," you are actually encouraging your workers to gripe and complain and to carry out the directive with a less than whole-hearted effort. The success or failure of many management directives depends on the supervisor's willingness to present them in a favorable light to workers.

Supervisors also have a responsibility to communicate upward. Management wants and needs to know how well workers are doing their jobs and how workers feel about their work. One of the primary concerns expressed by workers is that no one listens to their problems or does anything about them. Employees' problems and concerns can be resolved only if management addresses them. However, management (or the governing body) must first become aware of the problems. It is important that workers feel that their supervisor is concerned about them and is willing to express their problems for them.

You should give thoughtful consideration to the means you use to communicate information upward. It can be done face to face in a meeting or one on one by telephone. Or, you may decide to put information in writing, in a memo or letter or formal report. Time, importance of the information, its accuracy and its sensitivity all weigh upon the means of communicating the information. If having an accurate, permanent record of the message is important, for example, putting it in writing is essential. However, if confidentiality is important, then communicating the message in person may be critical.

In any event, it is important to be prepared. Plan what you intend to say and decide how best to say it. Organize your information—whether it represents facts, ideas, or impressions—so that it is clear and understandable. Present the information in the way that you feel will best accomplish your purpose.

Some supervisors think that if management knows the employees' concerns it reflects poorly on them as supervisors. They feel they aren't doing a good job. However, many problems and issues cannot be solved at the supervisory level. Legitimate employee concerns should be communicated upward for the benefit of both employees and management.

Summary

It is easy to see why communication is so much a part of good supervision. Communication is the process supervisors use to get work done through others.

Supervisors must be aware that they do not communicate merely by sending out various types of messages—these messages may have little meaning in themselves because messages are merely symbols of meanings. If a receiver does not attach the same meaning to the message that the sender does, no communication occurs between them.

As we have said, effective communication is a two-way process. It requires a willingness to change or to be changed—essentially, it demands an open mind. We have to be willing not only to express ourselves but also to hear what others have to say and to give their messages thoughtful consideration.

Good communication between supervisors and workers can help the work group function better as a team in completing tasks. And good communication can help the supervisor gain the trust and respect of workers—something that is basic to developing effective supervisory practices.

Checklist

Be aware of the difference between communication and effective communication.

Recognize that communication is a process and involves a number of parts.

Understand the various ways of communicating verbally and nonverbally.

Learn to use both the formal and informal channels of communication in your organization.

Recognize the major barriers to effective communication.

Understand the importance of giving and receiving feedback.

Remember the significance of good listening in effective communication.

Appreciate the relationship between good communication and good supervision.

PLANNING WORK
AND TIME

There is nothing so useless
as doing efficiently
that which should not
be done at all

Peter F. Drucker

Chapter 6
PLANNING WORK AND TIME

How can you get work out on time?

How do you distribute work fairly?

How can you best manage your time?

How can you keep stress out of the working day?

You probably know a few supervisors who always look as though they had a tough day at the office (or the yard, or the station), like people in the television commercials for upset stomachs. Their employees either do the wrong things or do the right things the wrong way. These are often supervisors who will have everyone on overtime one day, and on the next day have almost nothing for their employees to do. The work in their units is all right sometimes and not good enough at other times. And it is often late. You can almost see them going home and arguing with their families, or spending half the evening trying to unwind.

And yet these supervisors may in fact be as intelligent as their more successful counterparts. Have you ever wondered why their days are so complicated and unproductive? Much of their problem may be not lack of intelligence or basic ability but lack of planning—planning of both work and time.

Before you became a supervisor, you were responsible only for your own work. But now you are responsible for seeing to it that all the work assigned to your team is done on time and properly. A multiplier effect is working on you. Since you are now responsible for much more work, planning is more important than before. If you don't do a good job of planning for and with your work team a lot more can go wrong. Also, as supervisors, some of you are probably finding that because of interruptions and the demands made on you by other people, you often have less time than you need to do your job and do it well. And this may be causing you stress.

Good planning of work and time can help you stay on top of things, have more time to do those things you must and want to do, and reduce stress.

What is planning?

For supervisors, planning means deciding *what* must be done, *when*, and *by whom*. It also means scheduling your time and the time of your employees, as well as scheduling the use of equipment, materials, and everything else needed to get a job done well and on time. And it may involve changing the way work is done. Some supervisors plan in their heads and tell their employees about the plans in group meetings or by talking to individual workers. This may work well for some sit-uations, especially if the planning is simple and the job is small.

In most cases, however, written plans work better. They cannot be forgotten, everyone can look at them from time to time, and everyone can see whether the work is moving along as it should.

Whether a supervisor develops written plans or not, good planning is a "state of mind." It is based on a supervisor's recognition and acceptance of the fact that the clearer the idea one has of what one is trying to do, the greater the likelihood that it will get done. And good planning helps to clarify for everyone involved what needs to be done, in what order, by when, with what support, and by whom.

A good plan should have the following major parts:

A clear statement of the specific goals to be accomplished and the order in which they are to be reached

A step-by-step description of the tasks that must be done to reach these goals

A schedule for the people, supplies, equipment, materials, and space needed to reach the goals

A description of ways in which progress and results will be measured.

Studies have shown that good planning gets good results. Supervisors of teams that produce a great deal of work spend much more time on planning than do those whose work groups have low production rates. These same studies show that work teams with high production rates think of their supervisors as very good planners.

How is a plan made?

The main steps in making a plan are described in this section. They are: stating goals, streamlining the work, listing tasks, scheduling resources, and checking on the progress of the work.

Step 1: stating goals

Stating goals helps focus the attention of both the supervisor and the work team members on the specific projects and tasks they must accomplish together. Goal statements should answer these questions: What must be done? Where must it be done? By when must it be done?

To illustrate, think back to the goal statement used in Chapter 3: "Complete properly all curb and gutter work [*what* must be done] on the north side of the 1400 block of Oak Street [*where*] no later than 4:30 P.M. on Friday, 15 November [*when*]."

You will also have to decide which goals are the most important, or which have to be

Planning: what must be done . . . when . . . who . . . how.

reached before work can begin on others. Stating goals clearly and setting their sequence or priority is the first step in any effective work plan.

Good planning also means breaking a goal down into tasks, subtasks, and activities that must be performed in order to reach that goal. Supervisors and work team members should work together deciding how to schedule these steps and listing the order in which they should be done.

Step 2: streamlining the work

Fast cars and planes are streamlined in design so that they can move forward using the least amount of energy possible. Perhaps your work can use streamlining, too. Is there anything that is done in your work unit that could be done more easily? With fewer steps? In less time? With less effort or fewer people or materials? How might the work be simplified? How might it be done more easily, cheaply, or efficiently?

Ask yourself—and ask your employees—the following questions at this stage:

Which jobs or parts of jobs could we eliminate or simplify without harming the quality of the work?

Which activities could be combined to save time, effort, materials, or space?

How could we change the way work is done in order to improve efficiency? Could we change to a new or better machine? To more useful forms?

Step 3: listing tasks, subtasks, and activities

Let us assume that you are supervisor of Fire Station No. 1 in Hometown, Ohio. You have been assigned the following goal: Reduce fire losses by $25,000 in the area served by your station during the next fiscal year. What *tasks* would be involved in accomplishing this goal?

Begin by writing them down. Many local governments have printed forms that supervisors may or must use to plan their work. If yours does not, you will probably invent your own after a while. In the meantime a blank sheet of paper will do.

Your list of tasks might read like this:

A Increase inspection of homes in the neighborhood for fire hazards.

B Increase inspection of business properties in the neighborhood for fire risks and compliance with fire safety ordinances.

C Teach citizens in the neighborhood how to spot fire hazards, prevent fires, and report fires promptly and properly.

D Get more citizens involved in fire prevention and protection.

Most of the tasks you list will have to be broken down into a series of *subtasks*. For example, under task A you might have the following subtasks:

1 Assign station firefighters to inspect 10 percent more homes in the neighborhood.

2 Provide an updated fire safety checklist for building and housing inspectors to use when they are inspecting.

3 Give the police department a short list of home fire hazards. Arrange with police patrol officers to report any fire hazards they see in or around homes in the neighborhood in the course of their regular patrols.

4 Prepare short lists of home fire hazards for garbage and trash collection crews to use to report any fire hazards they see while they are working.

5 Ask school officials for permission to enroll interested students in a junior firefighting company. These students

can report fire hazards they see in the neighborhood.

After listing these subtasks under task A, do the same for tasks B, C, D, etc.

In carrying out the subtasks you have listed, you will probably need to break these down further into specific *activities*. Under task A, subtask 1, for example, you might want to list the following activities:

a   Brief fire prevention personnel, coordinate the additional inspections, and get information and forms with which to make reports.

b   Identify neighborhood areas that are high fire risks.

c   Survey these high risk areas.

d   Identify additional houses to be inspected.

e   Determine how many more personnel hours will be needed to conduct the additional inspections.

f   Check the effect of these extra inspections on the station's readiness to respond to fire alarms.

g   Schedule the dates and times of the additional inspections.

h   Check with the building inspector's office to make sure the extra inspections do not interfere with other inspections scheduled.

i   Schedule the station personnel who will do the inspections, making sure that the schedule fits in with duty hours, training time, and vacations.

j   Arrange to get any equipment that is needed.

k   Conduct the additional inspections as planned.

l   Follow up on inspections to see that hazards have been eliminated.

m   Report the results of inspections to the fire prevention bureau or to the officer in charge.

The same kind of activity list should be made for each subtask. Next, you should work out and assign beginning and completion dates for each activity and indicate who is responsible for carrying out each activity. When all this information is in place, the result is a plan of action.

Step 4: scheduling resources

Now that your work plan is finished, you will need to schedule the time in which you plan to use the equipment and materials and even the space to carry out that plan. But, most

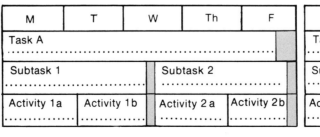 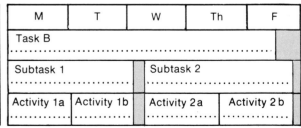

Work planning starts with a goal that is broken down into tasks, subtasks, and *activities that are scheduled by working days. Do not forget to allow for float time!*

important, you must schedule the time of the people who will be doing the work. You must make sure that your employees are not expected to be in more than one place at a time, and that the work load is evenly divided.

While you cannot always avoid conflicts with employees' personal plans, it is a good idea to talk to each employee before scheduling his or her time so that such conflicts come as infrequently as possible. Make every effort to resolve conflicts, but keep in mind (and remind your employees) that your first responsibility is to get the work done.

The staffing schedule is a key item in your scheduling of resources. Like a work plan, a staffing schedule needs no special form although some governments provide them or insist on them. First, list workers' names alphabetically down the left side of a sheet of paper. List the working days, for one week or more, across the top of the page. Be sure you include the month and date along with the day of the week.

When you schedule a worker for an activity that week, draw a dotted line opposite his or her name across those days on which the work will be done. (You can write the name of the activity on top of the dotted line to help you remember who is doing what.)

As the work gets done, show the progress of each job by making the dotted line solid. If the worker has worked two days and ac-

complished only what was planned for one day, mark only one day solid and extend your dotted line to allow more time.

This kind of chart (shown on this page) tells what each worker is assigned to do, how well the work is progressing, and when each worker will be available for new assignments. It also keeps you from assigning one person to do two jobs at the same time.

An equipment and materials schedule can be done exactly like the staffing schedule, by listing equipment and materials needed on the left-hand side of the page. Show under

the heading of days and dates when the equipment will be used and when the materials will arrive.

No matter how carefully work is planned, it is impossible to know when the unexpected will happen. Blizzards, flu epidemics, equipment breakdowns, and energy shortages are usually unpleasant surprises. But you can learn to expect the unexpected and to plan for it.

Experienced supervisors set aside a contingency day or two in the overall schedule to take care of unforeseen delays and compli-

	Jan. 2 Mon.	Jan. 3 Tues.	Jan. 4 Wed.	Jan. 5 Thurs.	Jan. 6 Fri.	Jan. 7 Sat.
Brinkman					inspection follow-up	----------
Carozo		inspection ----------				
Fine		in-service training - chemical fires --				
McCann	v a	c a	t i	o	n	
Phillips		inspection ----------			writing reports ----------------	

This simple activity chart can show you work progress as well as worker availability.

cations. You should have enough float time to take care of the unexpected but not so much that your unit becomes inefficient.

Of course, emergencies such as fires, accidents, and tornadoes may need more than extra time on your schedule. You should know in advance what you and everyone else in your unit must do if such emergencies arise (especially those that are most likely to occur in your area) and train your workers always to be ready. Indeed, they should be able to handle all emergencies whether or not you are there. This is one sign of effective supervision.

Elected officials often allocate a larger share of a local government's limited monies to those units in which careful planning is reflected in goals, tasks, subtasks, and activities that have taken schedules and dollars into account. While supervisors will not make major decisions about the department's budget, they can make a worthwhile contribution to it. If the supervisor involves them in planning, workers can also contribute.

Step 5: checking on the progress of work

An effective supervisor knows exactly where the work he or she is responsible for stands at any time. The secret of this lies in having a definite plan for checking *regularly* on the progress of work (Are we on schedule?), the accuracy and quality of work (Is the work being done right and done well?), and the

need for training workers (Could any part of the operation be improved by teaching new skills?).

You have your work plan. People, materials, and equipment are scheduled, and you have helped your department head set up a realistic budget. Everything is moving along as it should. Or is it?

To find out, you should ask yourself the following questions at the end of each day. Make a chart, if you like, or simply list these points on a piece of paper as a reminder to yourself.

Has all work scheduled for today been completed?

What has to be carried over?

Why does work have to be carried over?

Will it be necessary to make changes in tomorrow's work schedule (or the whole week's schedule) to get today's unfinished work done?

What changes should be made to avoid this delay in the future?

Is all equipment operating properly?

Did all the supplies come in as scheduled?

Will there be any absences from work this week that were not in the plan?

Has everything been done that I committed myself to do or check on today?

What should I give special attention to tomorrow?

Were there any tasks, subtasks, or activities completed today earlier than scheduled? How will this affect tomorrow's work?

With practice you will find that you can zip through this list at the end of the day in a few minutes, checking *every* item as a way of getting ready for the next day.

When you have finished your checklist you will know whether the work is on schedule and you are ready for tomorrow. And even if work is not on schedule you know what is wrong and what must be done to get back on the track.

One thing to bear in mind is that effective supervisors check on the progress and quality of the *work*. They do not check on the workers themselves. Employees should feel that you trust them if you are going to earn their respect as a team leader.

Managing your time

The demand for more services and lower taxes is perennial for cities, towns, counties, and other local governments. You may feel there is never enough time or money to get any job done right—that you are always pushing harder and harder to meet deadlines, while more and more work is pouring in. And you may be right.

Although little can be done about the demand for services or the lack of funds, there is something you can do to lighten the load on yourself. You can learn to use your time more wisely and more effectively.

It may surprise you to know the results of some studies of the work which supervisors do. These studies show that most supervisors spend only about 20 percent of their time on the activities that produce 80 percent of the results. The rest of their time—80 percent of it—is spent on work that has little payoff. Think of how much could be accomplished, and how much wear and tear you could save yourself, if that 80 percent were used more productively.

To start, you might do the kind of work planning described earlier. State your goals clearly, and then put your time where your priorities are. Concentrate on doing those things that help your team get results and reach goals.

Next, keep a log for one week to see exactly how you are using your time. Every hour write down what you did during that hour. After five days review your log carefully and ask yourself: Did I use my time in a way that helped my team to reach its goals? What kinds of time traps do I often fall into?

You might notice that you spend a lot of time talking on the phone. Or maybe a lot of your time is taken up by people who just "drop by to chat."

Once you have pinpointed how your time is being used, you can take steps to save time. For example, if too many phone calls are too long, try jotting down the main points you want to discuss before you make a call. Be friendly on the phone, but businesslike. End the conversation when you have finished discussing what you planned to talk about. Do not go into social chitchat on the phone unless you believe that socializing will help your team achieve its goals.

If you find that a lot of your time is taken up by people who drop by, then control this situation by *scheduling* your appointments. And when you cannot control the drop-in visitors, do not be afraid to tell some of them that you are sorry but you are very busy at the moment—that you can see them another time. Then *schedule* an appointment with them.

If the people who drop by are members of your own work team with questions or problems, it may mean that you are not using your supervisory time wisely. You may be spending too much time in your office or doing paperwork. You might plan to "wander around" more frequently where your team members are working. While you are doing that, you may be able to accomplish a number of things: You will be available to your

team members if they have any questions or problems, so they won't find it as necessary to drop by your office with their inquiries or concerns. Perhaps you can do a little coaching or skills development, showing members of your team how and where to work "smarter" to produce better results with less effort. And very importantly, you may catch your people doing well so that you will be able to praise them and thus encourage them to do even better. If you can see how things are going, answer questions and help solve problems, and do some coaching and developing and motivating—all in the same short period of time—you really are managing your time well.

Plan into your daily schedule some time for "unexpected interruptions." Then, even if some of your time is taken up unexpectedly, you will still be able to accomplish the things you planned to do. It is also a good idea to schedule some time for "housecleaning" and getting yourself organized—time, that is, for cleaning your desk top, putting papers back in files, and organizing your own paperwork. If you allow for time to get things in place so that you can find them easily, you will save time whenever you need information.

Finally, practice the art of delegating "how to do it" authority to your employees. Chapter 4, on leadership, discussed this in detail. Remember that you must invest time in training and developing workers so that they will be able to answer their own questions or the questions of others. If you find yourself spending a lot of time telling workers how and where to make the next move, you will want to reread Chapter 4 especially carefully.

If you are confident that you and your team have planned the work carefully and have made provisions for the unexpected; that the work is progressing in accordance with the plans; that your work team is developing steadily in competence and self-control; and that your team members are well motivated, there is little likelihood you will find your supervisory responsibilities stressful.

Checklist

Make your plan before work begins.

Remember that the purpose of planning is to get the results you want.

Remember that effective supervisors spend much more time planning than less effective supervisors do.

Be sure to start with a clear statement of goals.

Decide with your team what must be done, where, and when.

Try to simplify the work and avoid unnecessary steps.

Clarify—by listing them—your tasks, subtasks, and activities.

Schedule the basic elements needed to achieve your goals: people, equipment, materials, money, and space.

Plan for emergencies, and expect the unexpected.

Check regularly on the progress and quality of the work that is being done.

Manage your time by putting more of it into activities that will get multiple results.

ORGANIZING FOR RESULTS

*And God created
the Organization and gave It
dominion over man*

Robert Townsend

Chapter 7
ORGANIZING FOR RESULTS

How is your local government organized?

How is your work unit organized?

How can you organize your workers into a team?

What supervisory style helps you become the leader of your team?

Good organization is what it takes to make things work. It means that all parts or pieces have been put together in the right way so that the finished product functions smoothly and makes sense. This is true whether you are assembling a jigsaw puzzle, a bicycle, or a group of people in a work situation. That is why you need to know two basic things about organizing people in order to have the work done as effectively as possible.

First, you need to understand the different ways in which systems such as local governments are organized. This will show you what the alternatives are and will give you the advantages and disadvantages of each. Then you will have a better picture of how your work unit fits into the organization of your department, and how your department fits into the organization of the entire local government.

Second, you need to know something about the ways by which you can organize people in your unit into a team and how you can keep that team going. This information will help you become the kind of supervisor who can turn a group of individuals into a *team* of productive workers.

Formal vs. informal

As you know, any organization chart shows how the people in that organization are supposed to work together—who is responsible for what, who reports to whom, and how each person is expected to relate to everyone else. It also shows how one unit is supposed to work with all the other units in the government or business.

This is called the *formal* organization. It tells us on paper what the chain of command is and what the areas of responsibility are. For example, your government may be formally organized into departments, which operate under a city manager. Each department may be run by a department head, and, according to this formal plan, you are shown as the supervisor of your work group.

While it is important for you to know and understand the formal organization of your unit, department, and government, it is equally important for you to know that another kind of organization also exists. This is called the *informal* organization, and it may be quite different from that shown on the organization chart.

The problem, of course, is that you cannot really make people work together in a certain way by putting their names in boxes on a chart. People respond to other people for their own reasons: because they like or dislike them personally; because they go to the same church or bowl on the same team after work; or because they come from the same small town in Arizona.

You have probably seen this sort of thing happen many times. A local government, for example, hires as chief of police a person who was previously chief in another local government. The new chief brings into the department several officers from the other local government's police department. Because these newly hired officers have known and worked with the chief and each other earlier, they probably will be closer to and therefore more influential with their chief than will other officers of the same rank in the current department.

Thus the informal organization may have nothing to do with the worker's rank or the department he or she works in. And the grapevine, which is the communications system of the informal organization, may not be transmitting the same information as the formal newsletters and memos do.

How can a work unit function when these two very different organizations operate at the same time? The answer is given in the second part of this chapter, which talks about teamwork. In a well-managed local govern-

People will not stay put on the organization chart—the formal organization chart, that is. The real challenge is to bring the formal and informal organizations together.

ment, in which people work as a team, there will be very little difference between the formal and informal organizations—between the way things are and the way they are supposed to be. People work well together in their assigned roles in spite of their personal feelings and friendships.

We will return to that subject, but first let us consider some of the models of formal organizations and explore their advantages and drawbacks.

Types of organizations

The major models of formal organization are:

Line organization, or chain of command, which is the simplest type

Line and staff organization, which is similar but uses experts to advise line officials

Functional organization, in which each of the organization's specialized functions has its own department headed up by an expert or specialist in that function

Program or project organization, which calls for a different arrangement of personnel for each project that the organization works on.

There are, in addition, several other organizational models. For example, internal security in a larger police department typically would be organized in a *parallel* model. The police officers assigned to internal security would report to the chief through a separate chain of command from that of the rest of the department. And "management by objectives" is a *systems* model for organizing to do work.

But most local governments are organized using the functional model, with separate departments for fire, police, public works, personnel, finance, and so forth.

While a local government might be organized functionally, particular departments of that government might be organized using other models, for example, line or line and staff.

Line organization

Authority flows directly from the top in this military type of organization. People get their orders from those above them through a chain of command. Everyone at the same level of authority does approximately the same kind of work and has about the same amount of responsibility.

Because this organization plan is simple and direct it is often used by small police and fire departments. The person at the top has complete authority, and everyone else's authority and responsibility is spelled out clearly. A police sergeant has more authority and responsibility than a corporal and less than a lieutenant, for example. All lines of responsibility are clear-cut; therefore, discipline is relatively easy to maintain, there is little confusion about who does what, and orders can be carried out quickly.

But there are disadvantages. While the top person has the benefit of complete authority, this can be a tremendous burden because it means being an expert in all phases of the work—from purchasing to personnel. This means that key people are hard to find and are hard to replace when they leave. Also, communication between people and between departments is often difficult in line organizations because everyone is expected to go through formal channels.

For example, if you are at the lower level of one division and you want to pass along an idea to someone who is at the lower level of another division, officially the message is supposed to go up your chain, over to the other chain, and then down that chain of command, even if the person is sitting across the room from you. You must make the suggestion to your supervisor who passes it up the line to the head of your division. The head of your division passes the idea on to the head of the other person's division, and it then goes down the chain of command until it reaches the person across the room. (The same process would be involved in coordinating the work of different units.) Of course, in actual operation informal or "unofficial" communication is frequently used to facilitate the passage of information through the organization.

Line and staff organization

This form of organization is different from line organization in only one respect: staff experts advise the person at the top. These advisers—whether they are personnel specialists or financial experts—have no line authority except in their own offices.

An advantage of this system is that it gives top management the help of experts in making difficult decisions. It is also more flexible, because the experts often communicate with the organization without going through the formal chain of command.

A disadvantage is that conflicts often arise between the advisers on the one hand and the line officials on the other. The personnel adviser may, for example, favor one policy while line officers favor another.

Functional organization

Specialized departments are set up in this type of organization, each headed by a specialist. In government, for example, these specialized departments might be fire, police, building and housing inspection, public works, finance, and personnel.

This form of organization works more efficiently than the line and staff method because the experts are not merely advisers, they are in the chain of command dealing directly with problems. But an important disadvantage is each department's tendency to think of itself as more important than the others, or to forget that it is part of the government as a whole.

Program or project organization

In this type of organization people are assigned to a project because of the particular skills they have, regardless of the department or unit of local government they happen to work in. Once the project is completed an entirely different set of people may be assembled to work on the next project.

Each project is headed by a different project director. While people are working on a particular project they report to that project director instead of the director of their regular department.

This type of organization is usually used along with the line, line and staff, or functional types. It is particularly useful for special projects, such as construction projects not put out to bid, which may not fit under one particular department's responsibility but may require the services of several departments.

Of course, there is no hard and fast line between any of these different methods of organization. All of them can be useful in certain situations and most governments use some combination of them all. For instance, the local government itself might be functionally organized into specialized departments, while the police and fire departments might be organized on a line basis. In addition, the line and staff method might be used, for example, in the case of the city attorney advising the mayor.

Organizing for supervision

Many years ago a management expert tried an experiment in supervision. He realized that supervisors had a great many duties to perform—too many, perhaps—so he decided to make each supervisor a specialist in only *one* of the duties normally expected of a supervisor. One supervisor was in charge of seeing that the proper amount of work was done, another checked on the quality of the work, a third handled only record-keeping chores, and so on.

Needless to say it didn't work. After Supervisor A told a worker to speed up production, Supervisor B told her to slow down so that she could do a better job.

The management expert found that no person can serve two masters. It is a basic concept of life and of organization also. It means that each worker should have only one supervisor and that all supervisors should know which employees they are responsible for.

Of course, supervisors can do an effective job only if the number of employees they supervise is neither too large nor too small.

Supervisors who are responsible for very large numbers of people can do little more than oversee—like the captain on the bridge watching the deckhands below.

On the other hand, supervisors who are responsible for only one or two people are likely to watch them too closely and not give them the freedom and responsibility they need. What, then, is the ideal number of workers for a supervisor? A number of management experts believe five to seven workers is about the right number for effective leadership, although this number may vary somewhat depending on the nature of the work being done, the physical separation of workers, and various other factors.

Many studies suggest that five to seven people is the natural size of a social group. Apparently that number of people can relate to each other often enough and closely enough to form meaningful relationships. Since natural social groups form the basis for a working team, this seems like a good size for a work group.

Supervisors who must manage more than about seven employees should consider appointing subleaders to help them, since, when more than seven people try to work together, subgroups and cliques begin to form anyway. If they are not formally organized, they may make it harder to keep the group together as a team.

As a supervisor in local government, you may have heard something about "organization development" or "OD." Organization development is concerned with developing a healthy organizational climate, an organization in which people are recognized as the most important resource and which, as a consequence, is able to achieve "extraordinary results through ordinary people," to quote a current best-selling management book. Building and maintaining a true work team is a vitally important element in organization development.

Building a team

In most work situations you do not start out with a team. You start out with a group of individuals who are *supposed* to work with each other. That is what the formal organization chart says.

But the informal organization is there, too. What actually happens is that people spend most of their time with employees they like and avoid those persons they do not have much in common with. They form groups and personal friendships on the basis of age, sex, race, background, or interests. All the old-timers may be in one group, all the employees from a minority group in another, etc.

Your task in building a team will be to reduce the differences between the formal and informal organization as much as possible. Your

job is to close the gap between what is and what should be, so that workers begin to talk about "us" or "our shop" instead of "my friend and I" or "we" and "the others."

How, then, do you build a close-knit, highly motivated, productive work team? Six steps intended to help you are outlined below.

Step 1: show workers where they fit into the system

Many people do not know what goes on beyond their desk or work area. It is helpful for them to see how they fit into the whole department or governmental operation so that they understand why things are done the way they are, why certain things must be done or cannot be done, and what authority you, the supervisor, do and do not have. It is also helpful for them to understand how working in a complex organization, while it has benefits, puts certain limits on each worker.

Step 2: hold frequent planning meetings with employees

Try to set aside about fifteen minutes every day or two—or at least once a week—for a meeting at which you can plan ahead and also discuss how things are going. It is important, however, to see that these meetings do not turn into fifteen-minute lectures from you. Those fifteen minutes belong to all team members, you included.

The informal organization (on the left) is built on personal ties of friends, neighborhoods, age groups, and similar interests that are separate from the objectives of the work group. Team building (on the right) helps bring the informal and the formal organizations and their objectives together.

Be careful to see that the meetings do not waste everyone's time. Have an outline in mind for each meeting. Plan to talk about items that team members have suggested as well as items you yourself think are important. Some examples might be the following questions:

How are we progressing in getting our job done?

What problems are we facing?

What can we do as a team to solve those problems?

Is there anything bothering any of us? If so, what can we do as a team to work it out?

Is there anything the team leader can do to make the work better or easier for our team? To make the work more interesting or satisfying? Or to make the work situation more pleasant?

If any action needs to be taken as a result of these meetings, or if information is needed to clear up a problem, start the next meeting by telling team members what was done or what the team needed to know. Remember, however, that you should not run the meetings—you should merely guide them.

Step 3: set goals with your workers

All the employees in your unit should have some say about these questions: Where are we going? Why are we going there? What are the best ways for us to get there? It is your job to help your workers understand what specific goals must be reached by the team, and then to let *them* help *you* set other goals and find ways of reaching them.

Step 4: encourage workers to suggest solutions to problems

You are taking a big step toward gaining respect when you welcome suggestions, and an even bigger one when you welcome criticism and do not take it personally. Your employees will respond when you demonstrate that you want to make the work situation better and easier.

When an employee makes a suggestion, express your thanks even if the suggestion cannot be used. When an employee points out a problem, it is important not to be defensive and try to explain it away. Think about it. Investigate it. Above all, let the employee know you are checking it out and trying to change things for the better.

Then report back to the employee explaining what was done (or why nothing could be done) about the problem.

Step 5: let workers tell you things you may not like to hear

Just when the team seems to be coming together an employee may tell you something about you or the work situation that has been bottled up for some time. This may happen at a meeting or in a face-to-face conversation. If it happens, try to remember that in most cases it is better to get the facts out in the open than to have resentments and misunderstandings smoldering silently inside people.

Once the air has been cleared and members of the team have leveled with you and with each other, everyone can begin to deal with the situation and can arrive at a better understanding of it and of one another. And respect should grow from this understanding. They may not like one another any better, but respect and understanding are worth more than superficial friendship in a team.

Step 6: let team members help set standards

You cannot build or maintain a true team if some employees feel you play favorites or are unfair in any other way. If employees have a say in setting standards and in deciding how well workers are measuring up to those standards, complaints should be few and judgments should be fairer in your unit.

Allow team members to help you decide what the value of each member's contribution is or how good the performance of the team as a whole has been. And be sure that everyone has the team's goals in mind when these decisions are made.

Supervising a team

The right kind of supervision—that which involves a shared effort—encourages teamwork. One of your tasks as supervisor will be to take a long look at what you yourself are doing to create team spirit. What kind of supervisor are you? What kind of supervisor should you be? Let us take another look at the different types of supervisors and the effects they can have on workers.

First is the tough boss who thinks most workers are lazy. Supervisors who are like this feel that they have to check up on everyone constantly in order to get people to work hard and to keep production up. They expect workers to do just as they are told, with no questions asked.

Under this kind of supervision, workers usually do what they are told to do, but they resent every minute of it. And they seldom do more than just what they have been told to do. They work only when the boss is around and they slack off whenever they can do so.

As for team spirit, there probably is not much with this kind of boss. Workers tend to cooperate only with their friends. They usually do not cooperate with the others, nor do they work toward common goals. The only thing they may have in common is their dislike for their supervisor.

Then there is the kindly "sweetheart" boss. Such supervisors think of their employees as children. They want them to be happy and loyal. These supervisors tell workers how the work ought to be done and then praise them when they do as they are told. "Good, Shirley. Now that's the way I like it done." If the worker does something wrong, this boss may say, "Now, Shirley, that's not the way I told you to do it," and Shirley knows she has let the boss down.

The trouble with this kind of supervision is that it makes workers dependent on the boss. They look to the boss for direction and usually do not try on their own to improve their work. They do not make suggestions, nor do they think for themselves. You cannot build a team with all the ideas coming from a boss— even a well-liked boss.

Then there's the indifferent boss. Supervisors like this one do not like people very much. Or perhaps they do not have confidence in their own ability as a supervisor. Whatever the reason, they try to do as little supervising as possible. They spend most of their time on paperwork.

In such a situation the employees are not getting direction or guidance. They do not know what they are supposed to do; they do not know what their goals are or how to reach them. Morale and productivity tend to be low. Here, the employees are certainly not a team; they do not know how to work alone, much less how to work together.

The good supervisor does not oversupervise, undersupervise, or treat workers like dependent children. Effective supervisors who are building a team are probably doing the following:

Sharing decisions about planning and scheduling work with employees

Encouraging workers to give their honest opinions and suggestions about the work

Helping each member of the group to understand the work, to get personal satisfaction from doing it well, and to grow and develop on the job.

Under these circumstances, the group becomes a true team. More work is turned out. Members cooperate with each other and with other units of local government. They are capable, independent workers. They take responsibility for doing the work properly and for handling emergencies on their own.

Once you have reached this point you have successfully organized a working team. Your next job will be to keep this team together, to help it grow, and to help it turn out more and better work. This means leading your team—a very important function discussed in detail in Chapter 4.

Checklist

Understand the formal and the informal organizations in your department and in your work unit.

Check to see which of the major types of organization, or combinations of them (line, line-staff, functional, and project), are used in your local government and in your department and how they affect work in your unit.

Use the six-step method for team building.

Show workers in your unit how all of you fit into the entire organization.

Work with your employees in planning, scheduling, and assigning work.

Always keep employees informed.

Encourage employees to give you their honest opinions and suggestions.

Work with individual employees to help them understand their work, gain satisfaction from doing it well, and grow and develop on the job.

Practice a balanced style of supervision; do not oversupervise, undersupervise, or treat employees like dependent children.

MOTIVATING EMPLOYEES

Our chief want in life is somebody who shall make us do what we can

Ralph Waldo Emerson

Why do people behave the way they do?

How can you understand yourself
more fully?

Why do people sometimes act against
their own interests?

Why do people resist changes
that might benefit them?

What do people want from their work?

Why is the climate of a work group
important in motivation?

When we talk about motivation we are really talking about the amount of physical and mental energy that a worker is willing to invest in his or her job. Note that this definition of motivation covers three points:

Motivation is already within people. The task of the supervisor is not to provide motivation. What is important for the supervisor is to know how to *release* higher levels of motivation to do the work.

Different people are willing to invest different amounts of energy and enthusiasm in their work. Not everyone is a rate buster, an overachiever. On the other hand, not everyone by any means is lazy or "poorly motivated."

The return in personal satisfaction that an employee receives from an investment of energy in the job affects the level of that employee's motivation. In other words, a low return in need satisfaction results in a low level of motivation; a high return in need satisfaction results in a high level of motivation.

In supervisory staff meetings you may have heard comments such as these: "We could get a lot more work done if our people were better motivated." "If you don't have employees who are motivated, a work group can never do a good job." "The reason these people don't do a good job is that they aren't paid enough."

People state these "facts" so often that we come to believe they are true. We now know, after many years of research into human behavior, some revealing facts about how and why people work. Here are three important findings on what makes people do their best or something less than their best.

First, scientists tell us that whatever people do is done to satisfy a physical need (such as the need for food) or an emotional need (such as the need for acceptance, recognition, or achievement).

A second important point is this: raises, bonuses, or fringe benefits are not the only way or even the best way of encouraging people to do more and better work. Of course, a fair wage or salary and other benefits are necessary, but we have tended to exaggerate the power of money in motivating workers to perform. Instead, it is our understanding of and ability to satisfy workers' human needs that count most, because having the chance to satisfy needs is what motivates a person to get the job done—and done well.

Third, the attitudes workers have toward work and their jobs are to a substantial degree the result of the experiences these workers have had at work or in life. They may have *learned* that hard or quality work does not pay off.

What makes people work hard?

What kinds of personal needs are we trying to satisfy? As human beings we have certain needs which include those necessary to sustain life itself, such as the need for food, the need for clothing, and the need for shelter. Our needs also include, among other things, recognition for what we do, and the chance to do those things that we think are important and that we can do well.

Psychologist Abraham Maslow suggests that our needs fall into five categories shown on page 90 as a ladder of priorities. You should remember that the needs higher on the lad-

The needs levels of human motivation.

This illustration is based on the extensive work of Abraham Maslow, especially his book Motivation and Personality, *2d ed. (New York: Harper & Row, 1970); this ranking of needs has been highly influential in the field of management.*

SELF-ACTUALIZATION:
Full development of abilities;
creativity;
fulfilled personal life
ESTEEM NEEDS:
self-respect and the respect of others
SOCIAL NEEDS:
sense of belonging; group membership; love;
acceptance by others
SECURITY NEEDS:
absence of threats to life, health, and safety; orderly environment
PHYSIOLOGICAL NEEDS:
food, shelter, and clothing;
environment that sustains life

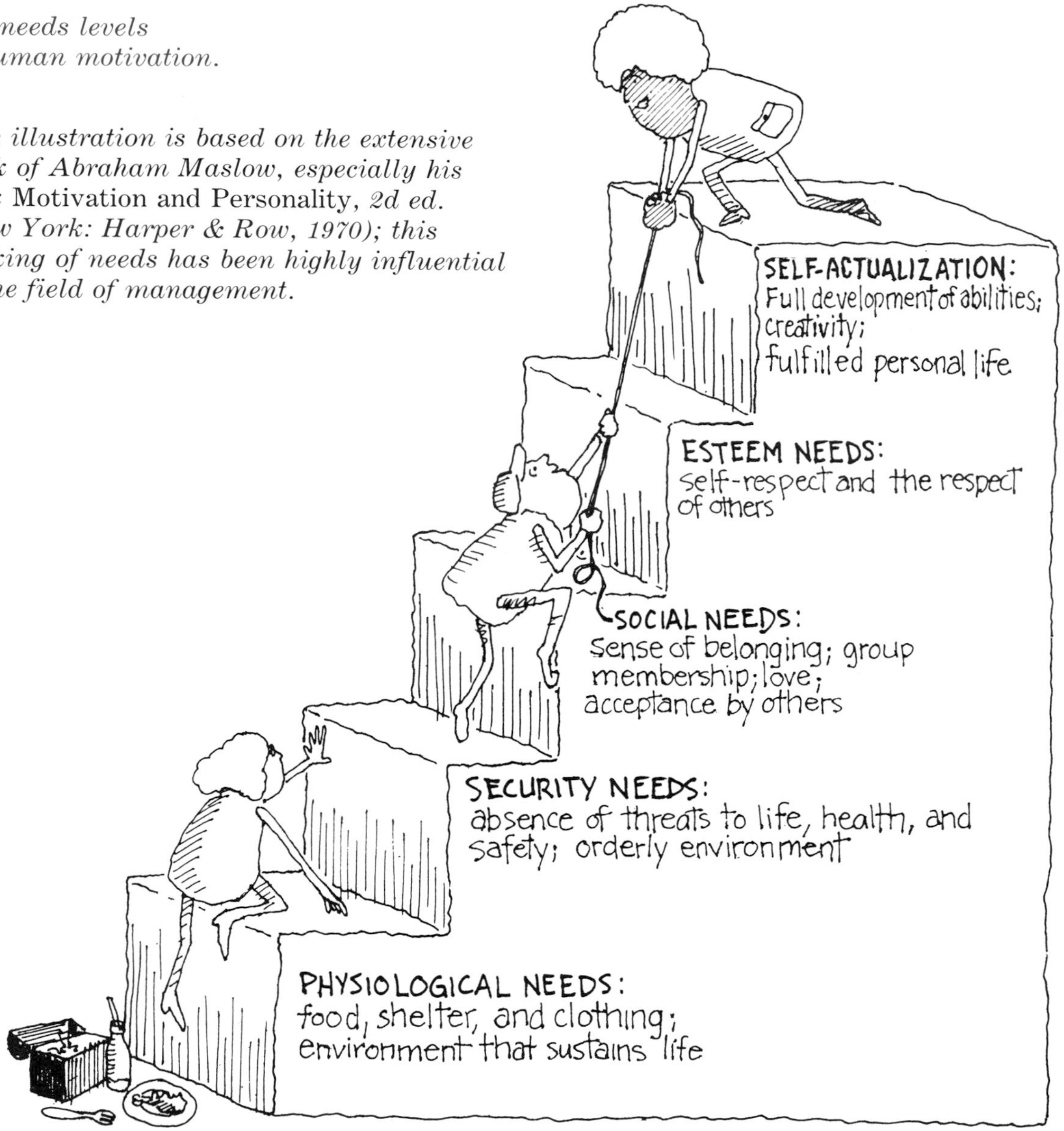

der are not more important than those lower on the ladder. It is simply that if a need lower on the ladder is not satisfied, a person will be motivated to satisfy that need first and will be "blocked" from releasing higher level motives. It has been said that Man lives for bread alone—when there is no bread.

Maslow tells us that when a person is truly hungry or really in need of clothing for warmth, that person will be strongly motivated to satisfy that need first of all. Once such bodily needs are satisfied, however, the person will seek satisfaction at the next level of need—the need for safety and security—until this level also is satisfied. Then the person is motivated by the next level of need, and so on.

The important thing which Maslow is saying is this: *once a human need has been satisfied, it no longer motivates a person.* For example, if a worker is able to satisfy all needs except the need for *self-actualization,* then what that worker considers most important is to be able to feel that he or she is doing something important that he or she wants to do personally, to feel that that activity is being done well, and, thereby, to feel fulfilled as a person.

When human needs are unsatisfied in the job situation, a person's work motivation will be at the lowest level at which there is an unsatisfied need. The supervisor's job, then, is to free this blockage in order to release higher levels of motivation in each of his or her workers.

Changes in the work situation—for example, a new and easier way of doing the job—may threaten some employees. They may be afraid of losing their jobs. Explaining the new procedures in advance and convincing these workers that there is no reason for concern will help satisfy their need for security and let them move to a higher level of motivation.

While Maslow's ladder of human needs helps supervisors to understand why most people behave the way they do, we also need to recognize that for some people the ladder has fewer than five steps. Many of us have heard about artists who aren't concerned with economic security or acceptance or recognition by others. Of course they need satisfaction of their bodily requirements for enough food, shelter, and clothing to survive. But their real motivator is their need to be creative and to fully develop their abilities. It isn't that such people don't have all five levels of need. Rather, it is that, for them, security and acceptance and recognition aren't very important needs. Their motivational ladder is a two-step one. Businessmen or investors who make a fortune in a financial venture and then invest everything they own in yet another venture provide another example. Certainly, they are highly motivated by something beyond the need for economic security.

Maslow's view that a satisfied need no longer spurs a person on brings us to a point that is important for all supervisors. Once a person's needs for a decent income and good working conditions have been satisfied, improving these elements of the job will cease to motivate the worker. This is an idea that many supervisors find hard to accept.

To satisfy the lingering doubts of many people, a number of studies have been made in different organizations. In one study both workers and supervisors were given a list of ten job-related factors. Supervisors were asked to rank these factors in the order in which they thought these were important *to their workers*. The employees were also asked to rank the items, in order of importance to themselves. In other words, both supervisors and workers were asked what workers want from their jobs. The table here shows how they answered that question. The numbers show the importance that supervisors and workers gave to each item (1 being most important).

Note that the factors the workers ranked 1–2–3 were the ones that the supervisors ranked 8–9–10!

Workers gave highest rank to appreciation for their work, being in on things, and sympathy for personal problems, while supervisors thought good wages, job security, and promotion would be most important to their workers.

Job-related factors	Supervisors	Workers
Good working conditions	4	9
Feeling "in" on things	10	2
Tactful disciplining of workers	7	10
Full appreciation for work done	8	1
Management loyalty to workers	6	8
Good wages	1	5
Promotion and growth in the company	3	7
Understanding of personal problems	9	3
Job security	2	4
Interesting work	5	6

Source: Paul Hersey and Kenneth H. Blanchard, *Management of Organizational Behavior: Utilizing Human Resources*, 3rd ed. (Englewood Cliffs, N.J.: Prentice-Hall, Inc., 1977), p. 47. Used by permission of Prentice-Hall, Inc.

Other studies have told us that supervisors often overlook the fact that most workers in the United States have enough of life's necessities and enough job security to be reasonably well-satisfied as regards both of these job-related factors.

Today many employees—especially younger ones, as discussed in Chapter 2—believe that having interesting work to do is of great importance. Many of us probably know people who work harder and better for their church or club or community as unpaid volunteers than they do for their employer who pays them for working. This is because they gain more satisfaction of their higher-level human needs from their unpaid work than they do from their paid jobs. Their volunteer work provides more motivators—interesting work or challenge, real responsibility, or personal fulfillment—than their employment provides.

The money we are paid for working is a hygiene factor (we need it to buy food, shelter, and clothing) but for most people it is not a motivator. Higher pay does not automatically motivate employees, especially those whose basic needs are met, to work harder or better.

A 1982 study that found that pay and benefits were ranked first among work values by clerical and hourly employees seems to contradict earlier studies, but it really confirms them. Unless the supervisor tries hard

Many workers are stopping at the second step on the Maslow ladder because they find more motivators in their personal lives than supervisors are providing on the job.

to provide motivators for these workers, they are unlikely to find much satisfaction in their jobs. When workers are not motivated by their work—when they do not find it stimulating or challenging or fulfilling—then they focus on other factors of the work environment, such as pay and benefits. Workers whose pay is low may focus on pay if they are not finding other motivators. In recent years, many supervisors and managers have been neglecting their responsibility to provide motivators for their workers. One of the important challenges for today's supervisor is to help workers find more interest and satisfaction in their jobs to fill needs for accomplishment and self-fulfillment.

The supervisor's role

The skillful supervisor, therefore, watches for each worker's needs, examines the extent to which they are being met, and then seeks ways of enriching the job to help each worker better satisfy those needs.

Your attitude sets the tone

For better or for worse, conditions in a work unit tend to reflect the personality and attitudes of the supervisor. Your own attitudes toward people in general are important because they will be translated into actions on the job.

In his book *The Human Side of Enterprise*, Douglas McGregor described some impor-

tant ideas regarding the attitudes of supervisors toward people. McGregor suggested that two different sets of beliefs about work and workers can lead to two different methods of supervising people.

The listings below present McGregor's two sets of beliefs. He referred to them as Theory X and Theory Y.

Theory X supervisors adhere to the following beliefs:

Most people think work is unpleasant and try to avoid it.

Most people must be supervised a lot and must often be forced to do their work.

Most people are motivated only by their desire for basic necessities and security.

Most people do not want to get ahead, do not want responsibility, and like to be told what to do.

Most people are incapable of thinking of answers to problems in the work unit or the organization.

Theory Y supervisors, on the other hand, believe the following to be true:

Work is as natural as play or rest. If workers think work is unpleasant it is

probably because of the way it is done in the organization.

Self-control in workers is necessary if work is to be done properly.

People are motivated by their needs for social acceptance, recognition, and a sense of achievement, as well as their needs for money to provide the basic necessities and for security.

Given good supervision, most people will accept and even seek responsibility.

Many people have the ability to come up with creative solutions to organizational problems.

It is easy to see why Theory X supervisors might use methods of getting the job done different from those used by Theory Y supervisors. Theory X supervisors think of workers largely as tools of production, motivated by fear of punishment or by desire for money and security. Supervisors with this outlook tend to watch workers closely, make and enforce strict rules, and use punishment and the threat of punishment as motivators.

Theory Y supervisors take an opposite view. They see workers as having varied needs. They see their own job as one of organizing and managing work so that both the organization and the workers can satisfy their needs. The Theory Y supervisor therefore works with workers to set goals for the unit, encourages workers to share in decision making, and strengthens workers' desire to do a good job.

Since McGregor wrote his book, research has shown that people really are more complex than either Theory X or Theory Y assumed them to be. Some people really are lazy and do try to avoid work, just as Theory X said. Other people truly enjoy working, as Theory Y held. Some workers must be supervised a lot, while others require almost no supervision. Some need to be closely controlled; others will control themselves more effectively than their supervisors can control them. In other words, there are Theory X workers and there are Theory Y workers. And there are some who behave according to Theory X one day, and according to Theory Y the very next day.

This research strongly suggests that supervisors need to understand not only McGregor's Theory X and Theory Y, but also a "Theory Z." Edgar Schein describes this "complex man" theory as follows:

People are complex, and also highly variable. They have many motives, which are arranged in a ladder of importance for them, and the order of importance changes from time to time and from situation to situation.

A person's motives interact with each other, and combine into a complex motivational pattern. A person might work hard for money, for example, in order to be able to spend a week skiing at Aspen.

People bring their motives with them to work. The experiences they have on the job teach them new motives. For example, people may come to a job strongly motivated to work. The experiences they have at work may teach them to dislike working.

A person's motivation is not the only element in determining how much work is done and how well. The skill of the person also is important. A highly skilled but poorly motivated worker may be as effective and satisfied as a very unskilled but highly motivated worker.

There is, therefore, no one correct supervisory strategy that will work for all people at all times.

Your actions release motivation

Regardless of how complex people are or what their prior work experiences have been, it is clear that if your objective is to release higher levels of motivation in employees you will need to do the following:

Enlist the help of workers in setting goals for the work unit.

Make rules and set conditions that help people get the job done, rather than hinder and frustrate them.

Regularly talk with and listen to other work team members to make sure they have a chance to tell you what they think.

Learn what "fuels" each team member's behavior; then positively reinforce behaviors that result in good work.

In short, today's supervisor must understand just what it is that makes each person tick and what is important to him or her.

Experience and research tell us that certain types of supervisors are better than other supervisors at releasing high levels of motivation in their workers. Successful supervisors usually do the following things:

They let their workers know that they are confident the workers will produce good work. They provide positive reinforcement of productive behavior.

They always praise good work rather than taking it for granted and noticing only mistakes.

They are easy to talk to and are willing to listen to new ideas. They try to make a worker feel good about making a suggestion even if the suggestion cannot be used.

They look at tasks, activities, and projects from the worker's point of view and explain to workers how their jobs fit in with the work of the whole department and of the entire local government.

They pay attention to how other people feel and correct workers' errors without making them feel discouraged, frustrated, or angry.

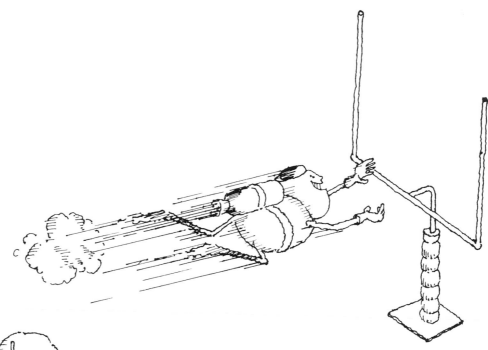

The job of the supervisor is to help release higher levels of motivation in employees.

This adds up to a healthy climate in the work group, and a healthy organizational climate results in high productivity and a high quality of work.

Let us now look at some specific supervisory actions that will help put this understanding to use—actions that will improve employee motivation, employee productivity, and job satisfaction.

One management technique that can be very helpful to supervisors in meeting this challenge is *job redesign*. Job redesign involves things like giving employees additional responsibility for planning their own work, allowing them to set their own work pace within broad guidelines, changing the types of tasks an employee does on a regular basis, or allowing more direct contact with the public. For example, you might ask an employee to set up a work schedule for a specific assignment with reporting dates that you will review together, rather than telling the employee when the work is due.

The motivators provided in this example would be at Maslow's fourth and fifth levels: recognition, and personal achievement and responsibility. We could provide another motivator at the fifth level, self-actualization through growth and learning, by giving an employee the opportunity to learn and perform new and more difficult and challenging tasks.

Another management technique that is sometimes used to provide motivation is *job rotation*. This involves asking employees to trade jobs for a specific period. It may involve cross-training, mentioned in Chapter 3. Job rotation is different from job redesign because you don't change anything about the job other than who does it. It can be helpful in motivating bored employees by giving them something new to do and broadening their perspective on what your work unit does. But if we merely substitute a job which contains few if any motivators for another which also has few motivators, rotation will not have lasting motivational value.

Supervisors must try especially hard today to develop and use the skills of successful supervision to motivate employees, because the 1982 study referred to earlier—a study of nearly 100,000 employees conducted by the Opinion Research Corporation—indicates rising employee dissatisfaction, which is a real threat to progress in productivity. While many managers and supervisors have gone back to a "tough" approach with their employees—perhaps because of recent economic conditions and tight budgets—getting tough appears to result in exactly the opposite of what these managers and supervisors expect.

Subsequent chapters in this book will help you understand how to develop and properly use supervisory skills to motivate good work.

Checklist

Accept the concept that motivation, like growth, is already within people. The task of the supervisor is not to provide motivation to others but rather to release and help channel the motivation that is there.

Learn how to recognize frustrations in individual workers and how to remove the causes, in order to allow each employee to move to the highest possible level of motivation.

Recognize that the assumptions you make about others affect your supervisory relations with them. Be sure your assumptions are correct.

Since many employees want more interesting and challenging work, learn how to make jobs more challenging. Be willing to spend time thinking about job changes and let your employees help in the thinking and planning processes.

Remember not to judge a person's ability on the basis of what that person is now doing. Most people are able to do much more.

MANAGING CHANGE
EFFECTIVELY

There is nothing more difficult to take in hand, more perilous to conduct, or more uncertain in its success, than to take the lead in the introduction of a new order of things

Niccolò Machiavelli

Chapter 9
MANAGING CHANGE EFFECTIVELY

Where do you get ideas for making improvements?

How do you decide where improvements should be made?

How do you choose a better way of doing things?

How do you get management, employees, and the public to accept new ideas?

If we listened in on some conversations between employees and their supervisors we might hear something like this:

"Why do we grind valves in the same old way?" asks Bill, the mechanic in the city garage. "I know the garage in Tannersville has a much faster, easier way of doing their valve-grinding jobs and they cut their costs by 20 percent. Why don't we give their way a try?"

"Do you know it takes three days to process an application for a building permit for a small one-story building?" asks Ann, a counter clerk in the building permit office. "A woman was in the office this morning. She wants to put up a building that is going to provide twenty jobs for people in this city. She was furious when she found out how long she'd have to wait for the permit! Do we need to make people wait so long to get an application processed?"

Effective supervisors know that suggestions like these from employees or citizens should be followed up by efforts to improve a service. Today, when cities have more people demanding more services, and fewer tax dollars are available, efficiency and economy are top priorities.

Listed below are four solutions that many supervisors resort to under the above circumstances. Which of them do you think would work best to save time and money for your group?

Let's ask everybody to do some overtime.

Everybody will just have to work a little harder and a little faster.

Let's get another set of tools and a new and bigger machine.

What we really need are two more clerk typists, a receptionist, and an answering service.

You are right: none of these suggestions is necessarily the best answer. All of them require that something be added: more work, more effort, more machines, more people, more money. But adding more of something does not always mean better service. The supervisor's first choice should be to get people to work *smarter*, not harder, and to make *better use* of the equipment and people already on the job.

This chapter deals with three important aspects of improving work methods: creating a climate for change, planning change, and implementing change.

Creating a climate for change

As a supervisor in local government you will constantly face the challenge of implementing change. The environments you work in today—political, social, technological, and economic—are changing, sometimes very rapidly. In order to be effective and to survive, governments must learn to adapt to change. The supervisor plays a key role in helping workers to respond and adapt to necessary changes.

The supervisor's most important task is to make sure that employees participate in every part of the change process. The suggestions, and especially the support, of your own employees is vital to the success of your plan. Failing to involve your employees can seriously hurt the morale of your unit.

If you have ever attempted to introduce a change in your work area you may have been surprised at the way people responded. You were trying to be helpful, to make life easier for your people. What you got in response to your efforts was anger, misunderstandings, work slow-downs, absenteeism, grievances—perhaps even deliberate foul-ups of the new, improved system. What went wrong? After all, you explained how helpful the change would be.

What you encountered was a normal human response to change. People are creatures of habit. We don't like to change our comfortable ways of doing things, even when someone we trust promises us the new way to do things will be better. Adjusting to the "new way" requires using some energy and will be physically and psychologically uncomfortable until the "new way" becomes a habit. Some people call this uncomfortable feeling while we adjust to change "stress."

There are many reasons why people resist change. Some of the most common are the following:

The "cost" seems too high. People believe (whether it's true or not) that the change will lower their income, or reduce their status in the organization.

People are afraid that they won't be able to learn a new skill required by the change and might lose their job because of it.

People do not trust the person introducing the change. This person may be considered an outsider or may be someone whose skills are not respected.

People don't understand the purpose of the change. People like to know the reasons for making a change. They want the change to make sense.

People really like the way they are doing things now. Most of us don't like to give up doing things we enjoy.

Peoples' basic values are challenged by the change and they are asked to do something they don't believe in or feel they must give up something they believe in.

People anticipate that they must give up their established patterns of friendship and get to know new people. If you like the people you work with, you won't like a change that makes you leave them behind.

For these reasons many people would rather live with a problem that is familiar than try to adopt a solution that is unfamiliar. As a means of self-protection many people will try to avoid the stress of making changes. If you insist that employees make a change that results in their feeling uncomfortable you may expect some negative reactions. Some of these negative reactions may be directed toward you, others may be directed at the change itself.

Among the people in your work group you may have some people who will strongly resist any change. They may actually be afraid to make changes. Other people may be more willing to try something new. They may enjoy the challenge that change can offer. To effectively manage the change that must take place at work you must know your people well enough to understand how each will respond. By understanding and anticipating their responses you can be more helpful to your people as they adjust to the new way of doing things.

Reducing stress

There are also some guidelines you can follow that can help reduce the stress caused by changes in the work place. When you are considering a change in the work place you must always consider what changes will occur in the lives of your employees and in all other people who will feel the impact of the change. This includes the public and employees in other departments of your organization as well.

You know that change creates stress and that the faster a change takes place the greater is the stress placed on the people involved. As a supervisor you need to consider: How fast does this change need to take place? Can it be introduced slowly or must it happen overnight? People will adjust better if the change can be introduced gradually. You should also consider how long the change will last. Is this change permanent or temporary? You should let your people know.

Some will change,
no matter what the obstacles.
Others will stay put,
no matter how bad the situation.

The greater the magnitude of the change the more stress and resistance it will generate. You should ask yourself: How different will things be after the change takes place from the way they were before? Can this change be made in small steps rather than in one big step?

We also know that people adjust to change much better if they know the change is coming and have some time to prepare themselves. You should therefore do your best to involve people in planning for change and keep everyone informed of changes that you know are being planned by others in the organization. You should ask yourself: What changes are coming that will affect my work group?

The stress of making a change is reduced if people know as much as possible about the change before it takes effect. You should ask yourself: Is there something I can do to educate my workers about the change before they have to implement it? Can I provide training in the new procedure? Can I send them to see this new piece of equipment in use in another department? Are there films or manuals that discuss the use of this newly designed tool?

We have learned that the greater the number of different changes that people must make in a short period of time the greater the stress they will feel. You may have noticed that your work crew begins to feel overwhelmed when asked to make many changes, even if the changes are small ones. You should ask yourself: Are we asking our people to make changes in other areas of their work environment right now? Do all these changes have to take place right now or can some of them wait? You will find less resistance to changes if you spread them out instead of piling them up.

Finally, we know that people will experience less stress if they feel good about the change they are making. People like to know why a change must take place. You should ask yourself: What can I do to explain the need for this change? How can I involve people in planning so they can understand why we need to make this change?

Sometimes organizational changes are mandated by someone above you and you are told to comply with the changes immediately. The principles of introducing change effectively must be violated and you know it will create stress for your workers. In these situations you can explain to your employees the reasons for the changes as you understand them. Giving your people a chance to talk about how the change is affecting them will help reduce some of the stress that the change creates.

Many times top management mandates a change in response to a crisis, not realizing the effect the change will have on the people who actually implement it. Since you are aware of these effects you can point them out to top management in a helpful way, out of concern for the organization's long-range success. After all, winning the battle but losing the war has never been sound management practice and we know that people under great stress are less productive. You could point out some ways to reduce the stress of making a change. Top management may be responsive to your ideas when they recognize that you are concerned about long-range productivity.

Involving your employees

As you introduce the need for change to your work unit and the public, you want to help people develop a *commitment* to change rather than force them into *compliance* with your demands. "Commitment" means people *want* to make the change. "Compliance" means people feel they *have to* make the change. Changes that grow out of commitment last longer and will work better.

Another equally important reason for involving people in the change process is related to effective problem solving. In most cases all of us together are smarter than any of us alone. Almost always the people who are actually doing a job will have the best ideas about how to improve the way the job is done. Supervisors frequently say that they could improve the way the government is managed if the administration would just listen to their suggestions. The same principle holds true for your workers. You need to listen to their suggestions and ask for their input in order to discover new and better ways of getting the job done.

Finally, people who have been involved in planning for a change that they must implement can enjoy the pride and satisfaction that comes with making a successful change. Things are working better now and it's because of their ideas and effort. Everyone can be proud of the group's accomplishment because everyone helped plan for it and do it.

There are many ways a supervisor can go about involving people in the process of change. In recent years "quality circles" have been used in private companies and local governments to get employees involved in solving problems. "Quality circles" involve the people who work on a task in the development of strategies to improve the quality of work done. A "quality circle" is not a "quick fix" solution to overcoming employee resistance to change. The basic elements of the approach are recognizing the expertise of workers, treating workers with respect, and involving them in planning for change.

Any approach to employee participation will work if and only if management is sincere about allowing *real* involvement and participation in planning for change. Management must realize that allowing employees to participate in planning changes means that management must be willing to share some of its power. If management is not sincere in involving employees in planning, resistance to change will undoubtedly occur. "Quality cir-

cles" and other participative processes should not be utilized as gimmicks to pacify employees. If a decision has already been made, or if management will only accept one decision, then this decision should be presented honestly to the employees.

Management that is truly interested in employee involvement will use the participative approach throughout the year. Since progress and growth require change, your employees should be constantly thinking how work can be improved. Don't wait for a crisis to occur before involving people in the change process. Continuous evaluation ("How well are we doing our job in the department?") will help identify potential problems before they become crises. Your employees will also know that their ideas are valued and respected. When change occurs they will be

Participation means teamwork. Everyone should help keep the ball in the air.

more willing to tolerate the stress of making the change. They will also be more willing to give the innovation a fair chance to work. They will be able to take pride in their success, and, last but not least, they will be less angry at their supervisor for implementing a change because they have helped decide what the change will be and how it will take place.

Planning change

In most cases when we improve the way we do a job we simplify it—we change it so that it can be done more easily, more quickly, and with fewer tax dollars. The following questions should be considered when you want to streamline the work methods in your unit:

Which methods need improving?

What are the steps involved in the job?

What is a better method?

Should this change be made now?

Which methods need improving?

Let us assume that you are the kind of supervisor who encourages employees to make suggestions and to discuss work problems with you. If so, you may have had complaints that the job is not set up as efficiently as it might be. (After all, there is hardly a job in the world that could not be improved by some streamlining.)

How do you and your employees decide which problems to tackle first? And which ones need most attention? The group will decide which are your most serious problems but the checklist below can help the group make a decision.

Does the work involve a large expenditure of money, worker-hours, or machines?

Does the job make up a large portion of the work load in your department?

Does the job involve many workers?

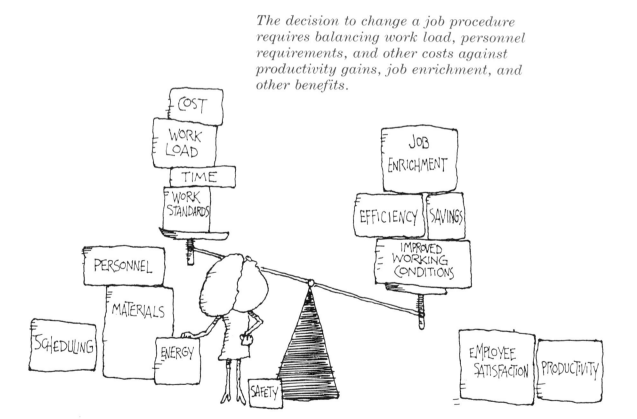

The decision to change a job procedure requires balancing work load, personnel requirements, and other costs against productivity gains, job enrichment, and other benefits.

Does the job involve a large number of highly skilled people?

Will the job last for a long period of time—more than a few weeks or months?

Do you often have trouble scheduling the job? And do you have backlogs, overtime, and missed deadlines?

Is the work produced not meeting quality standards?

Does the job result in numerous accidents or near accidents?

Does the work involve excessive physical exertion or tension, or require frequent rest periods?

Does the job create unpleasant or unhealthy conditions, such as unusual amounts of dust, noise, smells, heat, or cold?

Will change reduce tension, lessen fatigue, and relieve employees of the boredom of doing the same thing day in and day out?

Will change result in job enrichment for employees? Will it give them more satisfaction and a greater sense of worth and accomplishment?

Will change result in greater productivity, or better quality work, or a saving of money?

One final word of caution about choosing the job methods that need improving: Don't overlook the jobs that have been done the same way for a long time. The oldest methods may be the ones that need improvement most.

What are the steps involved in the job?

Once the group has chosen a job to work on, you want to take a closer look at the steps involved in getting it done. Remember that any job has three basic parts: the preparation part; the actual doing of the job; and the cleanup or put-away part. Preparation and cleanup are especially important to consider because they are often more time-consuming than the actual doing of the job.

Two helpful rules for breaking down the job into steps are: (1) Pick a subject and stick to it; and (2) Write a brief description of every step.

As far as the first rule is concerned, remember that most jobs involve a person, an object, or a printed form. When you make a study of the job, choose from these three the one that is most important to the job and then make a detailed list of what happens to that person, object, or form—where it goes, who handles it, how long each step takes. It is important to remember that if you start tracing the path of a printed form, for example, you should not leave that path to follow that of another printed form. In other words, stick with the subject you started with.

In writing a brief description of every step, you should physically follow the person or object you are describing. Do not try to do the job sitting at your desk. Bear in mind, too, that you should list all the steps in a job in the order in which these steps actually take place.

Keep your description brief and list only one step at a time. Do not combine two steps, using the word *and* in between. "She takes the form to Room 112 and then files it," should read: (1) "She takes the form to Room 112," followed by (2) "She files the form in the permanent file."

Whenever possible use action verbs and specific words that tell what actually happens: "Walks up two flights of stairs to the fourth floor filing room," is better than, "Goes to the filing room." "Types up information on four-page form," tells you more than, "Fills out the form."

Finally, record both time and distance for all steps. To get the time a job takes, watch it being done several times, time it, talk with the person who does the job and be sure this was an average situation, and then figure out an average time. In most cases time will be recorded in minutes and distances will be recorded in feet.

Here is a sample breakdown of steps involved in making an application for a building permit. The route of the application form was followed in the analysis.

1	Citizen fills out two page application form (10 min.).	
2	Clerk looks over application (5 min.).	
3	Form and plans are carried to inspection department by citizen (2 min./120 ft.).	
4	Form waits on inspector's desk (2 days).	
5	Form is checked by inspector (10 min.).	
6	Inspector writes changes needed on form and gives initial approval (20.5 min).	
7	Form is carried to clerk's desk (0.5 min./120 ft.).	
8	Form waits on clerk's desk (1 day).	

9 Clerk looks over form and discusses it with citizen (20 min.).

10 Clerk types permit for application (10 min.).

11 Application is filed (0.5 min.).

Total time: 3 days, 1 hr., 18.5 min.

Total distance: 240 ft.

In addition to making a list of the steps involved in doing a job, it is sometimes helpful to actually *see* the movements that must be made to get it done. A flowchart can be a commonsense means of showing them.

What is a better method?

When all the facts are down on paper—on a chart or a list—the group can begin to question and evaluate. Your most important asset will be an open mind.

Begin by challenging the job as a whole. Is the job necessary? Could the procedure be eliminated? Does it help accomplish work goals?

Next it is important to challenge every step of the job, to ask the group why. Why is it done at all? Why is it done at that time? Why is it done in that way? Why is it done in that location? Why does this person do it?

If the group feels the job is necessary, it can begin to think of alternatives—different and better ways of accomplishing the job. The discussion below, in the form of six questions, can help you in your evaluation.

Can we do away with the job or part of it? Doing away with a whole job or step is not easy, especially for people who have been doing it for a long time. But if the only reason given for doing it is "because we've always done it," you should certainly question the need for that job or that step.

Can we combine steps or jobs? Combining two operations will often save time and improve the quality of the work. You may be able to get rid of useless time between steps or you may be able to cut down some of the preparation and put-away time.

Can we change the order of steps or jobs? If parts of a job cannot be eliminated or combined they can perhaps be done in a different order. This can save time if it shortens distances between steps or if it gets rid of backtracking.

Can we change the place where the work is done? Too often work is done in a certain place just because it has always been done there. It may not be the best place. It may just be the place where the job got started. But changing the work location may make the work more pleasant and may save steps and time.

Can a different person do the work? Can someone else perhaps do some or all of the steps in the operation better or more easily than the person doing them now? Does the job need someone with different training or different skills?

Can we improve the equipment or the work environment? This should not be the first question asked, but it *can* be a way of improving work methods when all the other more basic and less costly changes have been considered. Purchasing new equipment without first studying and simplifying the job itself merely means that you are using poor work methods on a new, expensive piece of machinery. Quite often this "solution" can be more costly and more difficult to change than the problem you started with.

Should this change be made now?

Let us assume that you have studied your most troublesome job and have figured out why it was not functioning smoothly and how it could be improved. What do you do next?

Most changes take time and patience. Before you can begin the process of putting the change into effect you need to be sure that it is a change for the better and one that has a good chance of succeeding. At the very least it should not create more problems than it sets out to solve.

Check your proposal again to see that nothing has been overlooked. Does the new

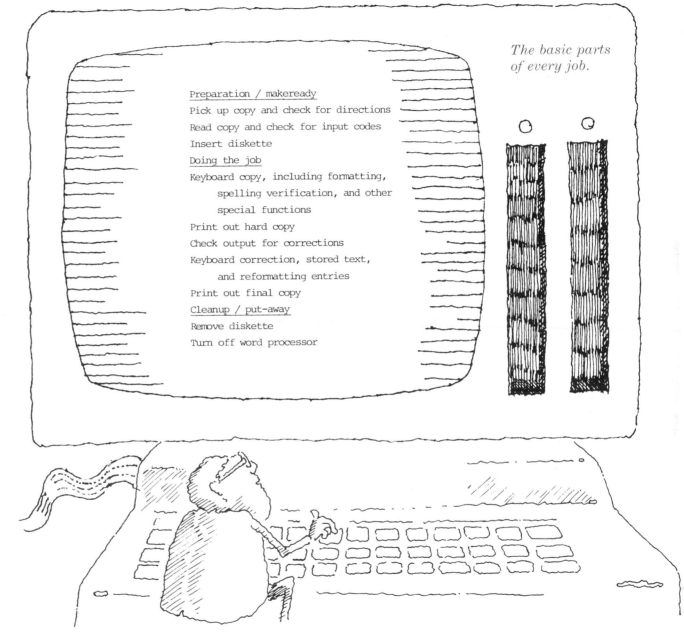

The basic parts of every job.

Preparation / makeready
Pick up copy and check for directions
Read copy and check for input codes
Insert diskette
Doing the job
Keyboard copy, including formatting,
    spelling verification, and other
    special functions
Print out hard copy
Check output for corrections
Keyboard correction, stored text,
    and reformatting entries
Print out final copy
Cleanup / put-away
Remove diskette
Turn off word processor

method comply with safety regulations? Is it in conflict with working conditions? Will it reduce costs? Increase service? Improve quality? Will the cost of installing the new method be offset by the lower cost of operation in the long run?

Remember, too, that you are part of a large organization. Have you thought of how your improvement will affect the work of other units and departments? (How would a change in meter readings affect the work load in the billing department, for example?) Is it compatible with other systems, schedules, and machines already in use in your department or government?

Timing is another important consideration. Have you thought about how the proposed change would be affected by recent public issues? What about the connection between your change and other recent changes in your jurisdiction? (You would not want to test your new method of installing storm sewers if most of the streets in the area were resurfaced a month ago.)

Do you have the money, materials, and personnel to make this change now? Or have you made too many other changes in work methods lately? Are you making changes more quickly than your department can adjust to them? Would it be better to make this change at a time when another department (or a department in a nearby city) makes a similar change?

Implementing change

When and if your new method is ready to be formally proposed, there are three groups of people you should take into consideration: those who must approve your new plan, those who must be consulted about it, and those who must be informed about it. Let us take a look at the human side of putting your idea across.

Getting your new method approved

You will have to develop a plan for obtaining managerial and legal approval to make the change you are considering. You will need to convince your immediate and perhaps higher level managers that your idea is a good, workable one. In a governmental environment checking the legal ramifications of a change is absolutely essential.

First of all, you should present your group's plan to your immediate superior and others in the chain of command, as necessary, pointing out both the benefits and the shortcomings of the plan. Be prepared to defend it— that is, to prove with facts and figures how it would affect service, schedules, costs, personnel, other departments, top management, and the citizens you serve. You may find it effective to have a small representative group of employees go with you to assist in making these presentations. These em-

ployees can respond directly to questions to help clarify your plan.

Be sure that you or your department head either checks or has the legal department check laws, ordinances, safety regulations, and timing, as well as other factors that might affect your plan.

In addition, explain to your department head how you plan to introduce your new method to other employees and citizens. Be sure you let your superior know that you are looking not only for approval but for suggestions that will make your plan more workable.

Informing your employees

Once the change has been agreed upon and approved you will want to announce it to the rest of the employees in your unit. It is important to be sure that everyone understands the reasons for the change and the improvements which can be expected.

Ask for questions and suggestions, but also answer the questions that may not be asked, for example: Will this change have any bad effects on me or my job? Explain, for instance, what the schedule for making the change is. Then ask employees if they feel it will give them enough time to adjust to the new situation.

If additional training will be provided, explain who will be trained and how it will be done. Will it be on-the-job training? Special training outside the job? Whatever it is, tell them about it; it will help them feel more confident about being able to handle the change.

If people will have to be moved around, explain that every effort will be made to keep them close to their former co-workers. And if the change is a major one it is important to avoid giving people the impression that the old way was completely inefficient. (Employees do not want to be told that they have been doing their work in an inefficient way for years.)

If a change is very sweeping or very threatening to many employees it might be well to take the "let's-try-it-and-see" approach by making the change a pilot program—an experiment to see whether something will work. It means that you expect problems but that the employees as a group will help identify those problems and will help solve them.

You will want to explain to employees that the success of the project depends on their willingness to suggest the changes that are necessary to make the project work. Sometimes it is useful to select a "team quarterback" to "call the signals"—the person on your work team who will do the best job of leading the unit in the new project.

Since a pilot project is an experiment, you will need to decide eventually whether or not the experiment has succeeded. Employees should keep the records you will need to compare the quantity and quality of the work done by the old method and the new.

When the "before and after" figures are in, employees should share in making the decision about the project. Did it save money? Time? Did it help us work faster? Better? Should we continue it? Change it? Or go back to the old system?

Answers to these questions should be written down in a final report for top management. If there is a difference of opinion on the results or the recommendation for action, you must include the opinions of the minority as well as the majority on your team.

Informing other employees and citizens

It is essential that you or your superior notify those who might be affected by your change: for example, employees in other departments who work with your own employees; council members; members of advisory committees; staff people such as the chief administrative officer, the personnel officer, the city engineer, the finance director, and the mayor.

If your project affects the public, you will need to let citizens know why, when, and how the change will take place, and how long it will last. This is usually done in coopera- tion with the administrative staff. For example, suppose you are planning to change the routing of several refuse pickup trucks. Citizens will want to know specifically why the change has been made, when the change will take place, how long it will last, and what the new collection dates will be. The time spent involving the community in your change will pay off in citizen help and support. (Chapter 17 discusses in detail the matter of communication with the public.)

Finally, some changes will require that special groups such as vendors who do business with the city, consulting engineers or architects, or county, state, and federal agencies be notified. You will want to discuss this matter with your superior and develop a communications plan.

Planning a follow-up program

An open mind is an important ingredient of any follow-up program today. Supervisors should realize (and should help their employees realize) that no change is really permanent. New techniques and new equipment are developed so quickly today that new ways can become outdated overnight.

An effective supervisor will encourage employees to continue to suggest new and better ways of getting things done. For example, the supervisor will continue to ask for suggestions at meetings and to circulate pamphlets, newspaper clippings, and other publications that may contain new ideas.

It is important to be receptive to suggestions. Suggestion forms and directions for their use can be placed near the work area. A committee should be assigned to review the recommendations every month or two and choose those that are most useful. Winners should be mentioned in your newsletter or on your bulletin board. They should receive a personal note of thanks from you as well as someone in higher management.

Indeed, everyone should know that his or her efforts are appreciated. Whenever a change is completed you can show your appreciation for your employees' support in one or more of the following ways:

By thanking them individually and in a group meeting

By writing them letters with copies to the personnel files

By recommending them for merit promotions or pay increases

By giving them public recognition in department, government, or community publications.

Employees who are praised for suggesting and making changes are likely to come up with other new ideas. At the very least they will not fear future change because they will think of change as positive and beneficial for government and for themselves.

Checklist

Involve your employees in every step of the change process.

Think about ways of getting people to work more efficiently before you request more personnel for your unit.

Think about new and better ways of using your equipment and supplies before you request more of them.

Choose carefully when selecting the job that most needs improvement. Do not overlook jobs that have been done in the same way for years.

Break the job down into steps and question each step when trying to simplify.

Check for safety hazards, legal problems, and other obstacles, such as those involving money, personnel, or time, before you choose a new way of doing a job or task.

Be sure you have the necessary approval before you make a change.

Explain new ways of doing tasks to everyone inside and outside of local government who will be affected by the change.

Follow up your change by evaluating whether it was worth making.

Let those who helped make the new plan work know that their efforts are appreciated.

Urge employees to continue to look for new and better ways of doing their jobs.

SELECTING, ORIENTING, AND TRAINING EMPLOYEES

10

*It is a fine thing
to have ability, but
to discover ability in others
is the true test*

Elbert Hubbard

Chapter 10
SELECTING, ORIENTING, AND TRAINING EMPLOYEES

What is the supervisor's part in selecting an employee?

How do you conduct a successful employee interview?

What steps should be taken in orienting new employees?

What should you consider in setting up a helpful training program?

Three of your most important tasks as a supervisor are selecting, orienting, and training the people assigned to your job area. You are more likely to get the job done with and through other people if your employees are carefully selected, are told what is expected of them when they start working, and are kept up-to-date by on-the-job training.

Selecting the employee

Today, in many cities, towns, counties, and other local governments, personnel departments screen people who apply for jobs. If this is the way people are hired for your organization it is your job to provide correct, up-to-date information to your personnel department. Do you, for example, furnish a current, accurate description for the job you

are trying to fill, especially if changes have been made recently in the job? Check your job descriptions to see if they state clearly and accurately the duties and responsibilities of an employee as well as the skills the employee will need.

If, on the other hand, you work for an organization that gives you some of the responsibility for selecting employees you should know how to conduct a job interview and how to prepare for it.

Preparing for the interview

You want an interview to go well so that you can get the information you need for selecting the right person for the job. But there is another reason for conducting a good interview: you are not only interviewing, you are *being* interviewed. Your interview will be that person's first contact with his or her new supervisor, and you will want that first impression to be a good one.

Get ready for the interview in advance. You will need time to collect information, to read the application, and to get your thoughts together. With good preparation you can use the interview time wisely and well.

First, spend some time looking over the person's job application, so that you will not ask questions that the applicant has already answered on paper, and also so that you will know what questions or topics have *not* been

covered and what questions do need to be asked during the interview.

Second, spend some time looking inside yourself to find out what your personal preferences are. Ask yourself, "What kind of person do I hope to hire for this job?" If your requirements are different from the qualifications listed on the job description, be sure you realize this. Keep in mind that equal employment guidelines say specifically that you must not disqualify a person because of race, sex, age, religion, nationality, or handicaps, or other personal characteristics that have nothing to do with the person's ability to handle the job.

For example, you may have stored at the back of your mind the notion that a good bookkeeper is a quiet person who wears conservative clothes. That means you will really be looking for a quiet, conservatively dressed person even though these requirements are never in the job description. (In fact, they may have nothing to do with being a good bookkeeper.)

If you look for your personal prejudices in advance, you can stop yourself from making an unfair, perhaps illegal decision about a person. When the times comes to decide, you should be able to say to yourself, "I like John. He is more neatly dressed than any of the others. But he doesn't have the education the job calls for. Susan's hair is rather disorderly and I don't like the way she dresses, but she certainly has better qualifications. I think we should hire Susan."

After you have looked through the application and have evaluated your own expectations, you will want to gather information that answers the following questions:

What skills will the worker need right away?

What skills can the worker learn on the job?

What personal biases and expectations should I guard against?

What questions shall I ask?

What topics do I want to discuss? In what order?

How long will the interview take?

Interviewing the applicant

Your interview will be more successful if you can accomplish the following four objectives:

Put the applicant (and yourself) at ease

Phrase questions so that they will give you the information you need

Listen carefully

Write down your observations promptly after the interview.

You and the applicant will learn more about each other if both of you are relaxed. Begin by introducing yourself. Use the other person's name right away, and continue to use it frequently throughout the conversation.

Try to create an informal atmosphere. When the interview begins, see that the applicant is comfortable. There should be no physical barriers, such as a desk or table, between you and the applicant.

You might begin by briefly reviewing a description of the job. This can also serve to supplement information about the job.

Avoid questions that can be answered by a yes or no, such as "Have you ever done this kind of work before?" "Do you think you can do this job?" The chances are that you will get a quick yes in reply. Ask, instead, "What skills do you think you have that would make you the right person for this job?"

You should also avoid questions that lead to obvious answers, such as, "Do you like people?" The applicant can hardly say no to such a question! If you want to know how the applicant really feels about people, ask, instead, "How would you handle an agitated taxpayer who comes storming into your of-

A person's dress, hairstyle, and other personal characteristics have nothing to do with his or her ability to handle the job.

fice about his garbage which has not been collected for two consecutive weeks?"

Most of us are so busy with our own thoughts while another person is talking that we often miss a great deal of what is said. But interviewing means hearing everything that is said as well as hearing *how* it is said. In other words, you should truly listen. To do this, you should see that there are no interruptions by people or the telephone.

When the applicant speaks, listen until he or she is finished. Do not begin to think about your answer until the applicant has stopped talking.

Do not worry about pauses in the conversation. It is not necessary to say something as soon as the other person stops talking. Give applicants time to gather their thoughts and continue with what they are saying. And give applicants a chance to ask questions about the job. They need a clear understanding of what is expected. Also, you can often tell a lot about a person by the kinds of questions he or she asks.

Finally, write down your thoughts about the applicant *as soon as the interview is over*, while the ideas are still clear in your mind. Use a standard form to record your reactions. Such a form will help you look for information on the same characteristics in each applicant, so that you can make fair comparisons. It can also guide you in choosing your questions.

When questioning an applicant, be sure that you and the applicant are talking about the same thing.

Orienting new employees

Job orientation is another of your supervisory tasks; it benefits the worker, yourself, and, in fact, the entire agency. An employee who is properly oriented is much more likely to become a productive worker.

The three main ingredients of a job orientation program are: discussing expectations, explaining and informing, and setting up a check-back system.

Discussing expectations

Early in the orientation period two points should be made clear: what you expect of the employee, and what the employee expects from the job. Sometimes employees quit or are fired because nothing they do seems to please the supervisor. However, these employees may not have found out until the day they left that they were supposed to volunteer for overtime—the supervisor had never told them that overtime was expected.

Misunderstandings can also arise if employees fail to mention their own expectations; then employees may become dissatisfied and disappointed with the job.

Since situations change, and expectations change with them, both supervisors and workers should continue to keep each other informed about what each expects from the other.

Explaining and informing

The new employee needs to know where things are, how things are done, and who does what. When orienting a new worker, give that employee a good start by taking the following steps:

Write down when and where workers should report to work on their first day, who will greet them, and who will give them their first instructions.

Introduce new employees to everyone they will come into contact with during the first week.

Give new workers a tour of the work area. Point out where tools, equipment, and supplies are stored, and where they will find restrooms, drinking fountains, places to clean up, and other offices and work areas they should know about.

Explain the rules and regulations of the organization—especially those that deal with safety, smoking and nonsmoking, parking, transportation, working hours, absence from work, work breaks, lunch hours, and paydays.

Give the new employees an employee handbook if your government publishes one. Set aside some time during the first week to explain important sections and answer questions.

Explain the steps employees must follow to clear up misunderstandings or get action on complaints.

Explain how supplies and equipment should be used, including the telephone system, typewriters, copying machines, and daily tools of the trade, and forms that are filled out routinely.

During the first week explain how each employee's job fits in with the work of the department and the local government. Show how the job, no matter how simple or small, helps provide services to citizens and is an essential part of a well-run organization.

Orientation will be expedited if you assign one or two experienced and helpful employees to assist each new worker for the first several weeks. Be sure that new employees understand that these persons have been assigned to help them and to answer their questions.

The first work assignment for the new worker should be a simple one, but the work should be useful. It should not be practice work unless the job is so hazardous that practice is necessary. Be sure to check back at the end of the day to see that the task that was assigned has been done correctly.

Setting up a check-back system

For the first three to six months the person on a new job is under some pressure. Everything—and everyone—is new and strange. Almost everything is being done for the first time. Most new employees have moments when they wonder, "Can I really do this job?"

The understanding, supportive supervisor will help new employees get adjusted by using the check-back system. This means setting aside time for the new employee to ask questions and time for the supervisor to tell the employee what he or she is doing right and what needs improving or changing.

The new worker needs this kind of check back at the end of the first day and the first week. After that, the supervisor can schedule a monthly review of the employee's work for the first six months at least.

This type of stocktaking keeps employee morale high. It reassures newcomers as to whether they are doing a good job. It also keeps them informed about the supervisor's expectations.

Setting up training programs

Training workers for their jobs and developing their skills and abilities are important responsibilities of the supervisor.

In the course of this training period it is a good point to remember that some employees may have unpleasant memories of their school days. Part of your job, then, will be to provide the climate for learning by endorsing training activities, encouraging employees to take advantage of them, and helping them in every way to grow on the job. It will be helpful for you to recall those training programs that have been most valuable to you and why.

You might discuss with workers some of the following benefits of on-the-job training:

It gives new employees information on how to do their work the way the organization wants it done.

It gives all employees a chance to find out if they are doing their jobs correctly. Incorrect or inefficient work practices can be changed before there is lasting damage or before the wrong method is taught to someone else.

It gives all employees a chance to learn new and better ways of doing their jobs, to use new, improved equipment, and to keep up with the rapid changes that are taking place in every line of work.

It gives all employees a chance to grow on the job through learning new skills and taking on added responsibilities. This also pays off in promotions and salary raises.

These benefits to employees can also be considered benefits to the organization, and they make the supervisor's job easier and more productive. Supervisors can spend more time on planning ahead and preventing problems if the routine work is handled by capable, well-trained workers.

In addition to providing the right climate for learning, you will probably have to do some of the training. In most organizations the supervisor has at least some responsibility for planning and designing on-the-job training programs and for teaching and evaluating them.

Planning the training program

There are a number of points you will want to consider in the early planning stages. You might begin by asking yourself the following basic questions:

What do I want employees to know or to do, and at what level of skill?

What skills should they learn? What attitudes?

How soon do employees need this training?

What do employees already know? What skills do they have at present?

What do the employees themselves think they need to learn? (Ask them.)

When you have answered these questions, then ask yourself:

What is needed to provide this training? Equipment? Tools? Teaching aids? Money? Instructors?

How much time will be needed? How should the instruction be scheduled?

Before you start designing the training program, remember that you are designing it for a group of adults. It is important to stop and consider what we know about how adults learn best.

How adults learn

Adults should be given information spaced over a period of time. The period between classes should be long enough to give workers time to absorb the material but short enough so that they will not forget it from one session to the next. Weekly one-hour sessions would be better, for example, than monthly three-hour sessions. Training sessions should be scheduled far enough ahead so as not to conflict with work schedules or personal plans.

In any training session, individual involvement is important. Such involvement may be as simple as a question-and-answer period, or as complex as large groups breaking up into smaller groups for extended periods of discussion.

The kind of training also determines the size of the group. For example, specialized job instruction might be more effective in small groups of two or three, to allow for an informal flow of questions, answers, and discussion. In training sessions on areas such as building communication skills, larger groups of up to twenty will provide the opportunity for relating to a variety of backgrounds and experiences.

People learn at a steady pace. But after a while they come to a point where they seem to make little or no progress. Do not become discouraged if this happens. Before long, you will find that your students will begin learning again.

Remember that adults learn best when involved in a process. Words can be forgotten quickly, but when words go hand in hand with actions—with doing and participating—your students are more likely to learn and retain.

For this reason, these training sessions should appeal to people's senses. People learn by hearing words; by seeing words, charts, pictures, demonstrations; and by doing things. Thus, you will want to plan for a variety of teaching techniques (where practical), including lectures, case studies, role playing, demonstrations, and discussions.

You might also use a variety of materials, such as blackboards, charts, graphs, slides, maps, films, and other visual aids. Some local

governments may have videotaping equipment. If your organization has a training officer, that individual can be very helpful in providing ideas and assistance.

In order to remember what they learn, students must have a chance to practice. Studies show that if there is no time to practice 55 percent of the instruction is forgotten one hour after a task is learned, 65 percent is forgotten one day later, and 75 percent is forgotten one week later.

Instruction should follow a logical pattern. It should teach steps in the order in which they are actually done on the job. It should progress from the easiest idea to the most difficult. This permits students to build confidence while learning easy material and prepares them for the difficult tasks ahead.

Following a logical pattern also means giving reasons for what is done. Explain why it is done. Show the connection between facts and the ideas behind them. Employees will remember *how* something is done if they know *why* it is done that way.

Adults also learn best if they are at ease. In fact, we could say that a tense, frightened person scarcely learns at all. It is important, then, to create an atmosphere in which everyone is free to make mistakes and can learn from mistakes without feeling clumsy or ignorant. Be at ease yourself so that employees will feel free to experiment and to ask questions.

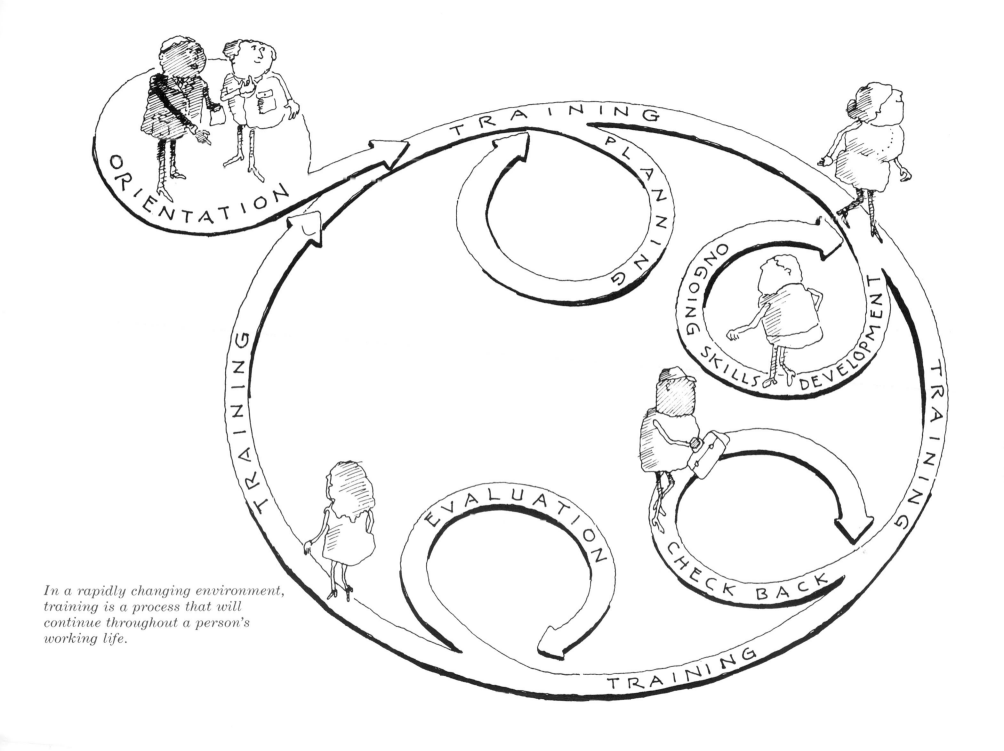

In a rapidly changing environment, training is a process that will continue throughout a person's working life.

Plan to hold training sessions in a place that has a pleasant, comfortable atmosphere. It should be away from the everyday work area, if possible, to provide a change of scene and to keep interruptions at a minimum.

Comfortable chairs and tables and adequate lighting should be provided. The room should be well ventilated, especially if people are smoking.

Other teaching tips

During the 1940s the Job Instruction Training (JIT) system was designed to train industrial workers quickly and thoroughly for work in plants geared up for the war effort. Some of the techniques used in the JIT system are as applicable to local government workers today as they were to industrial workers then.

The JIT system recommends teaching a task by breaking it down into its individual parts and then demonstrating it one step at a time. After each step has been demonstrated, provide time for questions and further explanation before going on to the next step.

A work sheet can be used to show the what, how, and why of each step in a task. The sheet would name the task and would show, step by step, what is done, how it is done, and why it is done that way. In addition, special tips about timing, safety, and efficiency could be added to the sheet.

It is often useful for supervisor and employees to trade places at this point. Have the employees tell you how to do each part of the task while you follow their instructions. Correct any mistaken ideas employees have about any part of the operation. And do not forget to praise them when they do the work correctly!

Then ask employees to explain the what, how, and why of each step and actually do the task. Watch for mistakes and correct them on the spot.

At the end of each training session it may be helpful to have employees summarize the key points that were learned while you write them on a blackboard or flip chart. You would then fill in any missing information and correct any misunderstandings.

After the employees are doing these jobs on their own, it is critical that the supervisor check back periodically to see how the jobs are being done. This provides employees with another opportunity to correct errors and the supervisor with an opportunity to give recognition for tasks done correctly.

After the training program has been completed it is important to try to measure what effect it has had. If the instruction did not accomplish all that it was designed to do, try to find out what went wrong so that the next program can be planned more successfully.

Ask yourself such questions as: Was the material too complex? Was it presented in an interesting, understandable way? Did the instructor use too many unfamiliar words? Did the instructor frighten or bore the employees? Were enough visual aids used? Was too much taught in too short a time?

If, as a supervisor, you are good at: selecting well-qualified employees; orienting new employees so they understand their responsibilities and feel comfortable with the organization; developing and maintaining a well-rounded training program—then you are well on the way to becoming a first-rate supervisor who elicits good work from employees—your most valuable resource.

Checklist

Have an accurate, up-to-date job description ready for hiring new workers.

Be well prepared for interviewing each applicant.

Be sure that you have clearly identified your personal preferences about people and how they relate to the qualifications listed on the job description.

Put job applicants at ease during the interview, and be at ease yourself.

When a new person is hired, state clearly what is expected on the job.

Listen to the new employee's expectations of the job.

Check back with the new employee regularly on job performance and on his or her reactions to the job.

Explain the written and unwritten rules of the organization to the new employee.

Encourage employees to participate in training programs.

After each training program is completed, carefully evaluate its strengths and weaknesses so as to enhance future programs.

COACHING
AND
COUNSELING

If you treat a man as he is,
he will stay as he is,
but if you treat him as if
he were what he ought to be,
and could be, he will
become that bigger and
better man

Johann Wolfgang von Goethe

Chapter 11
COACHING AND COUNSELING

Why is it important for the supervisor to act as a coach?

How can coaching improve your employees' performance?

Why is it important for the supervisor to be able to counsel employees?

How can you use counseling skills to help an employee solve performance problems?

We saw in Chapter 5 that many situations arise daily in which you can exercise principles of good communication. Coaching is applying good communication techniques to the work setting. The technique of coaching goes beyond issuing orders to your employees—it involves helping them learn and develop to the best of their abilities. In this sense your position as supervisor is similar to the role of a coach on a football or soccer team. It is a daily responsibility, a job that never ceases.

Counseling is a less frequently used skill, but one that is just as important to the successful operation of your work team. If you sense that one of your workers is personally troubled, unhappy in the job, or just not performing up to standards, some counseling

may be in order. Later in this chapter we will give some concrete suggestions about handling this sometimes ticklish subject. But first, let's deal with the everyday job of coaching.

What is coaching?

Coaching is helping your workers learn and do their jobs to the best of their abilities. It may involve on-the-job training in basic job skills, or it may involve more subtle motivation by which you encourage your employees and help them refine their skills and increase their job efficiency.

Coaching is one of the most important and challenging aspects of supervision. The successful supervisor, like the successful coach, can create a positive work environment by giving support and encouragement to others and by reinforcing their desire to do well. Like a good coach, the supervisor is able to get across his or her performance expectations. A good supervisory coach observes the team members, knows their abilities, and is able to bring out the best in them.

Given the fact that today's workers think of themselves as individuals and resist and resent being bossed, encouraging teamwork and at the same time recognizing individual effort is not an easy task. The supervisory coach knows when to lead employees, when to push them, and when to have the patience and tolerance to let workers alone.

Great coaches are known for their team building, their teaching, their planning, their perception, their strategies, and their leadership. Remember that it is not just game-winning decisions that make coaches successful. The hard work of successful coaching lies in helping a group of people to learn to perform as a team—that's the essence of coaching.

Those who fail at coaching usually don't fail because they lack knowledge of the technical aspects of the game. They fail because they can't translate their ideas and plans into action by their players. The best plans and decisions in game situations are useless if the players can't or won't follow them. Winning coaches are those who can direct players toward a goal that they themselves are interested in achieving. Players usually respond to coaches who show confidence in them. They are more likely to succeed in game situations when coaches have demonstrated day-to-day support and encouragement. The great coach assumes responsibility for teaching the players the skills they need—and for encouraging the players to excel.

There are times when the supervisory coach will be severely challenged. It may be by the educated subordinate who feels he or she is more qualified for the supervisor's position, or by the marginal worker who does just enough to get by, or by the employee who possesses excellent technical skills but is not able to get along with his or her co-workers.

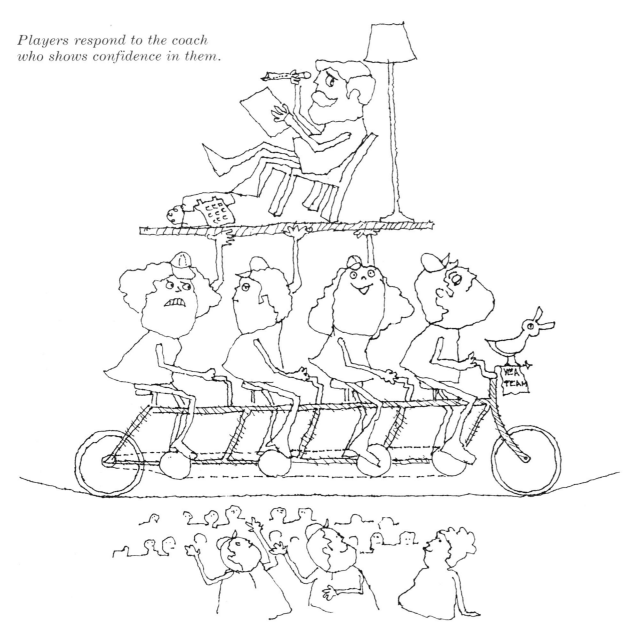

Players respond to the coach who shows confidence in them.

In the face of these challenges, the supervisor is responsible for getting the work out— for results and productivity. He or she must direct the individual's work and that of the crew or team, yet still have a vision of the big picture, the goals the department must accomplish. It is the job of the effective supervisory coach to find ways to cope with human demands and to inspire commitment from subordinates. After all, the true test of a successful coach is not only the day-to-day performance record—it is the bonds of trust and respect created within the team that produce consistent winning results over a long period of time.

The supervisory coach

Your actions as a supervisory coach can either encourage a subordinate to perform to the best of his or her abilities, or cause the subordinate to resent you and work against you. Effective coaching is in most cases the psychological aspect of dealing with people— not the psychology presented in textbooks, but the psychology of plain ol' horse sense!

It is important to remember that different coaching actions will almost certainly produce different reactions among your employees. No two people are alike. For instance, you may successfully correct one employee who has just made a mistake by mildly calling attention to the mistake and requesting that he or she try not to let it happen again. On the other hand, with a different employee, you may need to be much more severe and explicit in dealing with mistakes made.

The line in the song that says "different strokes for different folks" is a fitting lesson in coaching psychology. Knowing the individual, his or her needs, and knowing which of your coaching actions will be perceived by the employee as a reward or as a punishment is a very important aspect of coaching. A point to remember is that what serves as a reward or punishment for you, the supervisor, may not do the same for your employees.

An illustration of this is the older supervisor who comes to work in local government after a long military career. For a long time he has served in an organization where directives, orders, inspections, and discipline surrounded daily activities. He motivates his employees in the way that he is accustomed to being motivated—by using his authority and threatening punishment for wrongdoing. He may feel that most of his subordinates hate work and that they will try to get away with doing the least amount of work possible. Because of his attitude morale in the work unit falls, the employees resent him for his iron-fisted techniques, and they do only what they are told to do and not a bit more. This supervisor fails to realize that fear and threat of punishment can carry you only so far—and that if they do not produce the desired behavior once they are used, they

become ineffective management techniques (after all, what else can you do to the employee once he or she is fired?).

More important, he fails to realize that different people in his unit and different situations require different coaching actions. For example, one employee works well for him and is eager to learn new skills. However, once he learns them he becomes bored and his work deteriorates. In the place of threatening this employee with disciplinary action for poor work, an effective coaching action would be to point out to the employee how much the employee's eagerness to learn is appreciated. Then the supervisor can point out that the employee is having a problem staying with a job until it is satisfactorily completed. The supervisor lets the employee know how this problem is affecting the entire unit, and enlists the employee's support in finding ways to correct the problem. Successful coaching supervisors treat subordinates as responsible adults who can help find solutions to problems.

Effective coaching

The effective coaching supervisor builds a strong one-to-one relationship, or one-to-small-group relationship, with his or her workers. In football, for example, the real coaching takes place among the subunits of the team, such as the offensive linemen, offensive backs, defensive linemen, and linebackers. Nothing is more essential in di-

recting and motivating the activities of others than the bonds of trust and mutual support that develop in a strong one-to-one relationship. The coach must take a close look at each person and try to figure out: How can I get across to this person what I want done? How can I bring out this person's best work efforts? Then you must constantly evaluate what he or she has learned and how the new skills and knowledge are being used in the performance of the job.

Praise and encouragement are the most effective coaching tools. They enable the supervisory coach to define exactly what he or she expects of the subordinate in a *positive* way. Also, the good behaviors and performance of subordinates are reinforced through praise and encouragement. However, some employees may respond better to criticism—and it is the supervisory coach's responsibility to observe and see which workers may need praise and which workers may respond better to criticism.

Remember, though, that a person must possess a very good self-image before criticism can stimulate desired behavior. Most people want to know how they are doing and want to be told if they are not doing the job right. However, ineffective supervisors are apt to criticize a subordinate too harshly, or to focus criticism on the person rather than on the problem. Criticism should always be directed at correcting a problem, not at demeaning an individual's personality. For example, if a cashier in the tax department is wearing clothing inappropriate for the job, avoid saying, "Your taste in clothes is horrible for a person who has to meet the public much of the time." Instead, you might say, "I have a problem with the clothes you've been wearing lately on the job. I think that the taxpaying public may be put off by your appearance. Let's sit down and talk about how we can remedy the problem."

A good coach tries to be a "people developer"—and you can't develop people by tearing them down. The point to consider is that you need to direct your criticisms and actions at correcting the mistake or solving the problem, not at calling attention to defects in an individual's personality.

Think of a supervisor you may have worked for whom you considered to be effective. What characteristics of that person's coaching style do you recall? Do you remember how he or she treated you and how you felt? Some comments probably are:

"He was a motivator—I always found myself wanting to give my best."

"She was a diplomat—always tactful in letting me know what needed to be done or how I had messed up."

"A real smooth communicator—I never realized how hard he worked to have me understand exactly what he wanted me to do."

"She was firm, but fair—always treated everyone consistently and you knew exactly where you stood."

You may remember many other things about how you felt working for an effective supervisory coach. There are several coaching actions that contribute to effective supervision. They are:

Provide your employees with positive encouragement—employees will respond favorably when they feel they are being supported.

When you have to criticize, focus on the mistake or the problem, not the individual's personality. A problem-solving approach will result in less hostility and increased performance.

Give your employees both positive and negative feedback—they want and expect information about their performance. It will help them to develop and become better at what they do.

Build and maintain strong relationships with your employees—there is no substitute for face-to-face contact. Be accessible to them, and be attentive to their problems.

Confront employees with problems in their performance. Be honest with them about your feelings when their behavior is

unacceptable—a constructive attitude and a sincere desire to help the employee will help you increase the batting average of poor performers.

Listen more than you talk. Ask questions designed to give you information you need to solve the problem together. Don't ask a question if you are not going to listen to the answer.

Ineffective coaching

Have you ever worked for someone who was totally ineffective at supervising people? What characteristics of that person's work behavior made that person an ineffective supervisor? Some responses probably are:

"He took all the credit for the work *I* did!"

"She didn't take the time to really get to know people."

"She didn't think you had a brain and could think for yourself . . . she was always telling you where, when, and how the work should be done . . . she treated me like a child."

"He put himself on a pedestal once he made supervisor . . . you couldn't even talk to him."

"He was so unappreciative. He felt that you were paid to do a job and that you should just do it. The funny thing is that he was always complaining to me about how the department head didn't appreciate all the things he did to make the department look good."

Sound familiar? You may have thought of these and a number of other characteristics. In fact, you probably told yourself more than once that if you were ever promoted to supervisor, you would try your best not to be like that ineffective supervisor.

There are many specific supervisory coaching actions that can keep you from getting work accomplished through people—that can make you an ineffective coach. If you are on the receiving end of the following coaching actions, you probably react negatively and consider your superior an ineffective supervisor.

Threatening. "You better do this, or else . . .!"

Commanding. "You *must* do this!" "I order you to do this."

Attacking. "What a stupid thing to do!" "You've always been so lazy."

Moralizing. "Believe me, I know what's best for you."

Ridiculing or shaming. "You think you have it rough? You should have been around when I first came with the City."

"They just don't make workers the way they used to!"

Blaming. "You're the reason why so many things go wrong around here."

These coaching actions will almost invariably draw defensive reactions from workers. Think about it . . . if you thought someone was threatening you physically—say, going to punch you—what would be your first reaction? It would be to protect yourself; to defend yourself. Well, the same thing happens to us when we feel threatened psychologically. If we feel our well-being, our self-esteem, or our self-worth is being attacked, we are likely to react by protecting ourselves.

When threatened most people will defend themselves. For instance, if a supervisor threatens an employee with harsh disciplinary action the employee might deny that he or she has a problem or rationalize, making excuses for the undesirable behavior. The employee might counterattack by acting flippant or equally aggressive toward the supervisor. Or the employee might just take the threat of punishment and withdraw, like a turtle protecting itself from harm.

The sad fact is that productivity suffers, feelings are hurt, future work is jeopardized, and it will take a long time for the supervisor and the worker to patch up their relationship

after a conflict. The supervisor will probably label the employee a problem employee with a bad attitude. The employee, in turn, will probably be disgruntled and feel that he or she has been treated too harshly—and the supervisor may soon be looking for a new employee. However, an effective supervisory coach might prevent all this trouble from happening by developing and using a plan for coaching employees.

A coaching plan

Develop a coaching plan based on good coaching actions. Elements of a plan follow:

Let subordinates know what's expected of them by setting standards and clearly defining job responsibilities.

Let subordinates know how they are doing, through positive and negative feedback, evaluation of the workers' performance and documentation of their strengths and weaknesses, and a performance interview at least once a year.

Mutually develop a plan for improvement, by monitoring the employees' progress in areas that may be deficient and suggesting appropriate training. Recognize and praise performance improvement.

Basic coaching—
look at the employee—
measure the employee—
work with the employee.

Finally, remember the chapter on principles of effective communication. How you get your message across is as important as what you say. Your enthusiasm, eye contact, nonverbal behavior, gestures, voice inflection, all are powerful coaching tools at your disposal. You have the opportunity to convey encouragement, trust, and support, or to convey hostility, dissatisfaction, and disapproval. Don't lose the opportunity to be an effective supervisory coach!

What is counseling?

Counseling is another application of good communication principles that you can use on the job. Counseling skills can help you develop your employees and build a positive relationship with them. Most of all, counseling skills can help you be more effective as a supervisory coach. Most employees want to feel the sense of accomplishment and satisfaction that comes from doing a good job. They want your approval, and they want to be able to come to you for help. Counseling skills help you to capitalize on these needs. Employees can and do change through the supervisor's effective use of counseling techniques.

Counseling is a face-to-face communication or interview that can be used in a wide range of situations: for performance appraisal, for work progress review, for dealing with employees with personal problems, and for addressing employee performance problems. For example, counseling may be the first thing you do with an employee who wastes time, who has a record of being late or absent, who is careless, who has a drinking problem, or who seems to be going through a personal crisis at home. Think of counseling as the first step you take toward solving performance-related problems. Sometimes counseling is the step you take before taking disciplinary action.

The difference between coaching and counseling

The essence of counseling is that you:

Help your employee identify a problem.

Help your employee figure out alternative ways to deal with the problem.

Help your employee to arrive at a solution to the problem—or, if not a solution, at least a decision on what needs to be done.

Hold your employee accountable and responsible for the decision.

To do these things you must resist being judgmental about the person and the deci-

sion made and resist the temptation to make the decision for the person—you must avoid letting the person know what you would do. You can only hold the person accountable for correcting a problem if it is his or her decision to correct it.

This is what distinguishes counseling from coaching: when coaching, you direct the activities of others, while in your role as a supervisory counselor, you act as a reporter, an observer, someone who can help the employee to help himself or herself and to manage his or her own life better, without directing how he or she should manage—that needs to come from the individual. Most adults strive to gain more control over their lives and situations. Self-control makes us feel more secure and gives us a sense of well-being. If you put yourself in the position of making personal decisions for an employee, you are likely to damage that person's self-esteem. In effect, you are treating the person as a child rather than as a mature adult. Your role as a counselor is to try to help your employees solve their problems for themselves—they win because they experience more control over their lives, and you win because performance problems will be corrected!

Counseling skills

Counseling skills are behaviors a supervisor can use to help an employee find solutions to personal problems or other problems that

might interfere with work. The counseling skills that we will talk about here are:

Caring

Questioning

Listening

Understanding

Responding helpfully.

Each of these skills may seem obvious and simple, but they are not so easy to practice. To ask a question and really listen to the response rather than merely appear to listen, to really understand rather than to go through the motions of understanding, requires effort, concentration, and know-how.

While some people seem by nature to be more helpful than others, anyone who wants to be more helpful can improve his or her ability to care, question, listen, understand, and respond helpfully, by learning what to do and then practicing.

Why counsel?

It may be difficult for you as a supervisor concerned with output and deadlines to counsel with your employees and try to help them solve their problems. You might well ask yourself, "Why should I bother with counseling skills? I'm not a minister or a social worker."

A most obvious and important answer is this: Your position as supervisor gives you great influence in the work setting. In the same way that workers will look to you as their coach, they will look to you also for support, understanding, and direction in dealing with their problems of working and living.

If you can listen and be helpful in these situations you are also doing yourself a favor. When you take time to listen to and understand your employees, you are demonstrating to them that you are the kind of person they can talk to and trust. Therefore, they will be more likely to come to you with difficulties in the work setting while such difficulties are still manageable problems and not catastrophes.

Your department's productivity is affected by the attitudes and moods of all the workers. Workers who are spending time and energy worrying are putting less of themselves into their jobs. Similarly, workers involved in a misunderstanding with each other can disrupt the cooperation of the work team. The supervisor who takes a few minutes to talk over such concerns with workers is usually able to help relieve their minds and get them back on the track.

Taking an interest in your employees by showing them that you appreciate them and want to listen to them helps them to find satisfaction in their jobs. Recent studies have shown that these behaviors are far more important to workers than most supervisors realize. It should not surprise us. We all have the need to respect ourselves and have others respect and appreciate us. When you take the time to understand employees it helps to satisfy this need. Employees will usually repay you for your interest with loyalty and hard work.

Caring

Caring—or taking an interest in the worker— is any behavior on the supervisor's part that lets the worker know the supervisor regards him or her as an individual with rights, feelings, values, and a life outside the work setting. Caring is letting the worker know that the supervisor respects him or her as an individual.

Caring may be as simple as telling a worker he or she has done a good job or reassuring a worker that you know he or she can do it when he or she starts a new task. It can also be the following:

Going out of your way to tell a worker you are concerned when you learn he or she has had a death in the family, an accident, or some other upsetting event

---

Showing interest in and concern for people often is a simple thing to do.

Congratulating a worker who has been promoted

Asking a worker to show you a picture of his or her new baby or grandchild

Following through on a worker's suggestion or complaint.

A supervisor can also show caring in situations that are difficult or unpleasant. When a supervisor has to discipline a worker for a violation of a regulation the supervisor can ask to hear the worker's side of the story. When workers feel that a supervisor understands why they broke a rule and does not hold it against them, it is easier for them to accept that supervisor's warning or disciplinary action.

There are times when a supervisor must let a worker know that his or her behavior is affecting job performance and could result in dismissal. Again, if a supervisor is willing to listen to the worker and look at the situation from the worker's point of view, the worker may be more willing to hear the supervisor's recommendations. In the case of alcoholism, for example, a worker may be less defensive about the problem and may be more willing to seek help if the supervisor is understanding and helpful, not judging or condemning.

Caring also means respecting the workers. That does not mean the supervisor must *like* each and every worker. It does mean that the supervisor is willing to regard each worker as an individual with a right to his or her own ideas, values, attitudes, and life-style. This statement could be expanded:

Respect is listening to your workers and attempting to understand their viewpoints even when they are quite different from yours.

Respect is treating all employees fairly, regardless of their politics, race, religion, or appearance. It is giving yourself a chance to know people before you judge them on the basis of their hair, their politics or their skin.

Respect is accepting people who are different from yourself. It takes a person who is mature, who is satisfied to be himself or herself and is willing to let others be themselves. Remember that when people think or act in ways very different from yours, it can be threatening. You may take the difference as a criticism or mockery of beliefs that are important to you. You may feel threatened because you must take a second look at your own attitudes and beliefs.

An attitude of acceptance and respect for people *as they are* is essential if you are to be effective as a counselor. It allows you to be effective as a helper. It allows people to feel comfortable with you and talk about things that are difficult to admit, even to themselves. If your workers feel you will listen to them without judging them or holding what they say against them, they may be able to look at their problems more honestly, to admit more readily their responsibility, and to deal with problems more realistically.

Questioning and listening

One of the most important communication skills is listening. Listening to your worker and trying to understand what he or she has to say is a visible demonstration of your caring and respect for that person. In effective counseling, listening and questioning go hand in hand. Once you have asked a question and the subordinate is prepared to give you information, you should practice listening.

The supervisor should try very hard to listen and understand what the other person is saying. Hear the other person out. Don't interrupt. Be patient. Hear the other person's feelings as well as his or her arguments.

Use appropriate listening responses that convey to the other person that you are interested and want him or her to continue:

Show you are listening by facing the employee and looking him or her square in the eye.

A gentle nod of your head, with eyes fixed on the speaker, provides encouragement but does not necessarily indicate agreement with what is being said.

A casual remark such as "I see" or "Mmmm" lets the employee know you are following the conversation.

The use of questions closely relates to listening. It is what you do when you want the employee to provide you with further information, or when you want to clarify points already made. The skill is to be listening well enough to pick up key points needing further clarification without interrupting.

Important aspects of questioning are the tone of your voice and the phrasing of the question itself. Your phrasing and the tone of your voice will often influence the attitude and responses of the employee. For example, the following question is likely to bring about a very defensive or antagonistic response:

"Why did you mess up so badly on that report I asked you to do?"

A softer line of questioning focusing specifically on what you found wrong with the report is more likely to solve the problem. The supervisor could say: "I called you in here today to talk with you about the report you

submitted. There were some points I didn't quite understand. Also, you may need to check some of your calculations because I found some errors. Let's talk about how this report can be improved. First, did you have problems doing it?"

This problem-solving approach appeals to a person's sense of responsibility and maturity. You are more likely to solve the problem than if you humiliate or embarrass the employee.

You can ask closed questions, those which invite a one-word answer, such as, "Is that what really happened?" Or you can ask open, probing questions, inviting a more lengthy response, such as, "I understand you were involved in an accident. Can you tell me exactly what happened?" Above all, *don't* ask a question if you are not prepared to listen to the employee's response.

Understanding

Understanding is putting yourself in the other person's shoes, seeing the problem or situation from the other person's point of view. You do this by listening to the worker's words and feelings. As you listen, you attempt to think and feel with the worker and imagine what the situation the worker is describing *means to him or her.* Very often it is helpful to call on your own experiences to help appreciate what the worker is thinking and feeling. If a worker is describing resentment toward another worker, for example, you

might recall occasions when you felt resentment yourself.

Sometimes when you are trying very hard to understand someone you not only remember what the feeling is like but you actually go through that feeling along with the person. This is called *empathy* and can be very helpful to the other person. When you are feeling *with* a worker, everything about you—the expression on your face, the words you use, your tone of voice—tells the worker you really *do* understand just what he or she is saying.

Seeing a problem or situation from another's point of view can be difficult because each person reacts to a situation according to his or her own beliefs, attitudes, and past experiences.

Take the case of a parking ticket. You walk up to your car and see the red flag in the parking meter proclaiming "Violation," and under the windshield wiper is the parking ticket. The fine is only $1 if paid promptly.

Do you respond calmly and logically in this situation, recognizing that you are at fault, and take your $1 to the police station? Some people do—and some even find a bit of humor in the situation.

But there are also individuals among us who are outraged at being ticketed. They feel that the police should be tracking down muggers and burglars instead of ticketing parked cars.

Some people are angry at themselves for returning late, and some feel guilty when they think about their spouses finding out about the ticket. Some people are embarrassed at being caught violating the law. They walk up beside the car, glance around to see if anyone is looking, and snatch the ticket from under the wiper.

In each case, the situation is the same but people experience the situation differently. When you are trying to understand someone, then, you cannot take it for granted that they will react as you yourself would in the same situation. If a worker is promoted you probably assume that he or she is excited, proud, and happy about the extra money. It is possible, however, that the worker actually has mixed feelings, is worried about handling the new responsibility, or feels guilty about a friend he or she thought more deserving.

The only way you can be sure you have understood a worker is to check it out face to face. To do this, you can repeat in your own words what you think the worker is saying and feeling. If you have misunderstood either the facts or the feelings, the worker has a chance to tell you.

In your attempt to understand a worker, do not hesitate to ask questions about things that are not clear to you. Questions often tell a worker you are interested and want to make the effort to understand. Be sure, however, that your questions are important to an understanding of the worker's viewpoint. Questions that seem aimed at irrelevant details may tell the worker you are curious or inattentive rather than concerned.

The greatest blocks to understanding are our biases, prejudices, and stereotypes. We all have them. A person with an "open mind" is not someone without biases or prejudices. He or she is someone who knows his or her blind spots and works to keep them from interfering with understanding of another's viewpoint.

You can work to overcome your biases and prejudices, but first you must learn what they are. You can do this by noticing such things as the kinds of people you take an instant liking to, or by noticing the topics that you find it difficult to talk about without arguing.

Once you know your problem areas you can work on them. To fight prejudice, you can use your energy to understand another's point of view instead of thinking up arguments to support your own viewpoint. When you deal with a worker toward whom you feel prejudice you should look for the worker's good points instead of focusing on faults.

Responding helpfully

Responding helpfully is any action the supervisor takes to help a worker with a problem. It can be as simple as a word of praise or reassurance given at the right time. In some cases, the helpful response is listening and letting the worker know he or she is understood; in others, it may be helping a worker explore feelings that are difficult to face.

Responding helpfully often requires helping the worker sort through the alternatives he or she has to solve the problem. Discussing alternatives is different from giving advice or telling a person, "This is how you should do it." It involves talking over the pros and cons of different courses of action with the worker—and then leaving it to the worker to make the choice of what is best in his or her own situation.

It is not helpful to brush aside or minimize a worker's problem. In an attempt to cheer up someone who is upset, people often will respond, "Come on, now, it's not as bad as that," or, "You'll feel better after a good night's sleep." While these remarks are intended to be helpful, they usually leave the person feeling frustrated and misunderstood. When a worker comes to you with some difficulty, he or she is serious about it and he or she wants you to take it seriously.

Referring a worker for professional help

There are times when a supervisor will need to refer an employee for professional help. Employees who recognize that they need help for themselves or a member of their family may approach a supervisor and ask for a referral to an appropriate professional helper.

In other cases, employees may not voluntarily seek help but the supervisor may feel that professional assistance is needed. Referral may be necessary when alcoholism, emotional problems, or various other, similar, stresses are seriously affecting job performance.

In such situations the supervisor may have to bring to the worker's attention the supervisor's own knowledge of the employee's problem and its effects on job performance. The supervisor must then attempt to gain the employee's cooperation in seeking the needed help.

Remember that you cannot force an employee to seek help. Your role as supervisor is to:

Confront the employee with the problem and with how you see it affecting his or her work.

Advise the employee of any consequences that will occur if the behavior continues to affect work.

Recommend that you work together to see that he or she receives the needed help.

The following steps are intended to guide you in making a referral once the worker has agreed to seek help in this way:

Seek the worker's confidence by listening and by assuring him or her that you want to help.

Have as complete an understanding as possible of the worker's problem so that you will know which person or agency is the most appropriate source of help.

Encourage the worker to take part in the referral process by asking for his or her suggestions and talking over with him or her possible alternative sources of help.

Look for practical considerations, such as the worker's ability to pay for the services, whether the worker has insurance, medicaid, etc., to help cover expenses, or whether there are any difficulties with transportation or scheduling of appointments.

Learn as much as you can about the person or agency to which you will be referring the worker. Inquire about eligibility requirements for the professional service, fee scales, types of services, appointment hours, and similar essential information.

Make sure you are referring the worker to the proper professional person or agency. The worker will become discouraged if he or she is bounced from one office to another.

Offer to call the professional person or agency and make the appointment for the worker. The worker may be reluctant to make the initial contact.

Be sure the worker knows the name of the person he or she will be seeing in the office or agency. It is reassuring to the worker who walks into the bustle of an office or agency to know there is a person expecting him or her and willing to help.

Shortly after the time of the worker's scheduled appointment, check with the worker to see if he or she followed through on the referral. This lets you know whether the worker is making an effort to tackle the problem and lets the worker know you are interested in his or her progress.

The following agencies and other agencies like them in your community can probably help workers.

Community mental health centers (for people with emotional upsets; many operate drug and alcohol clinics as well)

Vocational rehabilitation services (for people with physical or emotional handicaps)

The U.S. Social Security Administration (for disabled workers)

Family counseling agencies (for parents having difficulties with children)

County children's services (for parents interested in adoption, or parents having difficulties with their children; such problems as runaway children and child abuse are also handled)

State employment services (for people changing careers or jobs)

Area adult vocational and technical schools (for people changing careers or jobs, or those interested in learning or updating skills)

Public health departments (disease detection clinics for heart disease, cancer, diabetes, etc.; family planning clinics)

Alcoholics Anonymous (nonprofessional group that provides support for alcoholics and their families).

For workers who want to seek help through psychiatrists or psychologists or counselors in private practice, the supervisor may contact the community mental health center and request the names of competent professionals in the community. The community mental health agency may also be a source of help or information for supervisors who have a question about whether they should approach a worker about referral for professional help, or who are having some difficulty in making a referral.

Confidentiality

If you are involved in a counseling relationship with a worker, *you are ethically bound to keep all your communications confidential.* You may not reveal to a third party what a worker has told you in trust and confidence, with two exceptions. One is in the case of a referral of a worker for professional help. In this instance you need to talk about the worker and his or her problem to the referral person or agency. However, you must secure the worker's permission to do this. The other exception is in the case of a worker who is a danger to himself or herself or to other people. In this instance you need to share the information with the proper authority or agency.

Checklist

Coaching:

Take an interest in your workers: show them they are important as individuals.

Use positive encouragement as the first step in coaching.

When coaching, focus criticism on the problem, not on the individual.

Develop a coaching plan—adapt your style and the plan to each individual and each situation.

What you say is far less important than how you say it—be aware of your tone, your inflection, and your body language—think how they affect other people.

Confront employees with problems in their performance. Be honest.

Listen more than you talk.

Counseling:

When you are listening to a worker's problem, give that person your undivided attention.

Give each worker the respect due everyone, regardless of beliefs, attitudes, race, religion, or lifestyle.

Put yourself in the worker's place and try to see the problem from his or her point of view.

Do not assume that a worker would react to a situation in the way that you would.

Help the worker explore feelings, since feelings are an important part of every problem situation.

Repeat what you think the worker is saying and feeling so that he or she can tell you if you have understood.

Help a worker sort through various alternatives to solve a problem; then let the worker decide which choice is best.

Do not minimize a worker's problem: he or she takes it seriously and wants you to do the same.

When a worker asks for professional help, or when a worker's problems are seriously affecting performance on the job, work with him or her to arrange referral for professional help.

Keep all communications between you and your worker in the course of your help strictly confidential.

EVALUATING
PERFORMANCE

*By the work one knows
the workman*

Jean de la Fontaine

Chapter 12
EVALUATING PERFORMANCE

Why do you evaluate work performance?

How can you conduct a work performance evaluation that helps both you and the employee?

How can you be sure your evaluations are fair?

How can employees be sure that evaluations are fair?

How do you conduct a formal evaluation interview?

Should evaluation affect salary?

What legal considerations will affect evaluation?

Almost all employees are anxious to know how well they are doing in their jobs, but many dread those sessions with the supervisor when their work is evaluated. It is like report card time in school. Many expect the worst and worry about it.

Most supervisors do not look forward to evaluation sessions themselves. Many feel reluctant to tell employees that they are not doing satisfactory work. Yet work evaluation is needed in government as it is in every other work situation. Does this mean that super-

visors must grit their teeth and force themselves to evaluate workers? Does evaluation have to be a nasty, unpleasant job?

Fortunately, the answer is no—not if it is done correctly. You should be familiar with your local government's personnel policy regarding evaluation. There are several types of evaluation systems in general use in local government today. Under one system the supervisor looks at a list of personal traits (such as dependability, cooperativeness, responsibility, creativity) and rates the employee from "unsatisfactory" to "outstanding" according to behavior on the job. Another system is more job-oriented: the supervisor measures an employee's work performance against a list of predetermined job tasks or objectives, which have been agreed to by both the supervisor and the employee. Other approaches combine elements of both these systems. While it is your responsibility to carry out completely the system your local government requires in its personnel policies, there is a method you may be able to use to enhance and expand the evaluation process, which will make it a less painful and more productive experience for both you and the worker.

What is this method? Briefly, it is a problem-solving approach to evaluation, as opposed to the older, critical, "here's-what-is-wrong-with-you" approach. Evaluation today is aimed at working out better methods of doing the job in the future instead of emphasizing and dwelling on what happened in the past.

This means that the supervisor is less like a judge and more like a coach, playing movies of the last game in order to show team members how they can score more points (or lose fewer) in the next game. Supervisor and employee are no longer on opposite sides of the fence, with the supervisor making accusations and the employee making excuses. The supervisor is on the employee's side. Both are trying to find ways to make changes that are needed and to reach goals both have agreed upon.

This chapter will discuss how this kind of evaluation works, but first let us address a more fundamental question: Why evaluate employees?

Why evaluate?

Evaluation of an employee's performance is expected and needed in local government for the following reasons:

Elected officials want evaluation because they believe it will encourage good performers to do better and will help poor performers to improve.

Department heads want evaluation to identify those who should be transferred to other work and those who should be promoted.

Other managers, and personnel officers, want information for making decisions on

If you make decisions based only on informal impressions of people, you will be wrong most of the time.

salary increases, promotions, and transfers.

Supervisors need a rating system for motivating workers or for making decisions about salary increases and additional training, among various other factors.

Employees themselves like to know how well they are doing in their work, how well their supervisors think they are doing, and what the future holds for them.

Formal evaluations are needed for another reason, one which is not as obvious but is just as important. Even if there were no formal methods, people would continue to evaluate each other's work without realizing it. The reason is simple. We all size each other up in a spontaneous, informal way as part of everyday living. Each person in a group has formed an opinion about the others in a group, although not formally evaluating those persons. But the difficulty is this: If supervisors make decisions on the basis of these informal impressions, they will be wrong most of the time!

Not only are first impressions frequently wrong, but often second, third, fourth, and even tenth impressions can be wrong as well. This is because we can confuse our own values, needs, and attitudes with the behavior we observe in others. In addition, we do not observe carefully enough when we make informal evaluations.

Because mistakes involving people's abilities are often very damaging and hard to correct, we owe it to others to conduct a careful, formal evaluation of their work.

Let us look at some general principles for making the kind of fair, constructive evaluation we have been talking about. Specific methods may differ from one local government to another, but the ideas behind them remain the same.

When do we begin evaluation?

We tend to think of evaluation as something that takes place toward the end of a period of time—the end of a week, a month, or a year. But it should begin the day a person accepts a job and a personnel file is opened. Into it should go a brief description of the job and the job specifications, the major responsibilities assigned to the employee, how the job fits in with others in the organization, and the new employee's qualifications.

During the first three to six months the supervisor should help a new employee understand his or her responsibilities, assignments, and authority, and relationships with other departments and people. Do not underestimate the amount of information and explanation new employees need. Most supervisors do not provide enough informa-

tion, while most new employees fail to ask enough questions because they are afraid to admit how much they may need to learn.

During this first half year, information about major work assignments, how well these are carried out, and any new information that comes to light about the person's abilities should be recorded in the files of a new employee. This should be shared with the employee.

Employees and the evaluation process

Evaluation should not be imposed on an employee from outside or from above. Employees and supervisors together should set goals, standards, and criteria for measuring employee performance.

Setting goals

After an employee has been on the job for about three to six months, goals for the next three to six months should be developed and stated. The employee should contribute as much as possible to the process at that stage. Of course, the supervisor must guide the goal-setting process to make sure that goals fit in with the realities of the work group, department, and government. But even an employee whose job is very precisely defined and limited can—and should—be given the chance to express the goals in his or her own words.

Among the goals set should be actions designed to fulfill the responsibilities spelled out in the job description. Goals should also cover actions—such as training or counseling—needed to help the worker meet these responsibilities.

Goals should be challenging but at the same time realistic. Supervisor and employee should agree that all the goals stated are relevant to the employee's job and are set forth in the right order of importance, and that enough time is available to reach them. The supervisor should be able to place this document in the employee's file with a feeling of confidence.

Specific goals for a three-month period for a police officer, for example, might be written down in this way:

Will report on time to all roll calls on duty days

Will participate in at least twenty hours of training

Will not have to be corrected about personal appearance more than once

---

Will not have more than two complaints regarding my language or demeanor from motorists given citations for hazardous moving violations

---

Setting goals is basic.

Will have car in proper working order and serviced when necessary

Will check interior of vehicle assigned to me at the beginning of each tour of duty for weapons or contraband which may have been concealed therein by arrested persons

Will advise all persons arrested by me of their applicable constitutional rights

Will know danger areas and trouble spots in my patrol zone

Will average writing one hazardous moving violation citation for each tour of duty

Will complete written reports with sufficient accuracy and thoroughness for 95 percent to be accepted without comment by the reviewing authority

Will appear on time and prepared to competently testify at all judicial proceedings for which I have been issued a subpoena

Will develop and submit information from four new informants on criminal activity pertaining to *Uniform Crime Reports* Part I offenses

Will submit one detailed written suggestion on how operations may be improved and the anticipated quantified benefits if the suggestion is implemented.

Setting standards

The employee now works with the supervisor to decide how well the job should be done—what will be considered satisfactory performance and how it will be measured. Employees may not agree with all the standards, but the fact that they have had some say in them will make for fewer disagreements or disappointments later on.

In any case, the supervisor has now placed in the personnel file information about the worker's job responsibilities and job qualifications, as well as a list of the goals which must be reached.

Evaluating performance

Many organizations schedule evaluations only once a year—on the anniversary of the worker's hiring, at the beginning of the calendar year, or at the start of the government's fiscal year. Unfortunately, this method does not work well because many of the actions that are discussed at an annual evaluation are old and perhaps forgotten, having taken place months earlier.

When an employee is told that he or she did something improperly eleven months ago it is too late to do very much about it. The supervisor simply finds fault with the worker, the worker feels rebuked, and no constructive action takes place. Perhaps the worker has repeated a mistake twenty times since last February. It is much better to point out a mistake (and improve the worker's performance) when it first happens.

That is why supervisor and employee should review goals frequently during the first three to six months. No fancy forms or complicated paperwork are required to show them where they are in relation to where they hoped to be. The right attitude on the part of the supervisor is far more important. Above all, the supervisor must be helpful and supportive. It must be clear in word and tone that the supervisor has confidence in the employee's ability and wants to help the employee get the job done correctly.

If the goals are stated clearly and the employee has kept good records of work done, the supervisor will not have to point out which goals have not been met. The employee will see this without help.

During this assessment process the emphasis must be on *results*—not on personality traits of the employee, nor the employee's shortcomings and failures. The employee should be praised for all jobs completed satisfactorily and on schedule. Next the supervisor should help the employee decide what the problems were when goals were not met, and how these problems can be overcome.

Finally, new goals should be set for the next three to six months. Notes on the new action plan should go into the personnel file along with information on how successful the worker was in reaching the previous goals.

The formal evaluation interview

Each supervisor should have at least one formal evaluation interview each year with his or her workers. When accompanied by periodic, informal discussions throughout the year to measure progress and give feedback on problems, an annual (or six-month) evaluation can be a valuable time to reflect on an employee's overall job performance. Discussing past performance and planning for the future can be a positive, constructive, and even enjoyable experience for both the supervisor and the employee. If a major improvement in job performance is needed, it is critical to have a formal evaluation interview. This evaluation process may determine whether any changes will occur in the employee's attitude and work habits. But it isn't easy. The ability to conduct a productive evaluation interview, particularly when an employee must make substantial changes or improvements in performance, requires careful planning.

Planning the interview

Start by reviewing your first evaluation of the employee's performance and consider your reasons for that evaluation. Your main objective in the interview should be to improve the employee's performance and motivation. Think about how you want to accomplish this. What is it about the employee's work that needs improving? How can it be done?

Picking the right day, time, and place is also important. The right place is a *private* place. The right time is not too soon after a disciplinary action. And the right day is one on which you are in a good mood and the employee seems also to be in a good mood.

Your responsibility is to be *for* the employee regardless of whether you like the employee and regardless of the kind or number of mistakes the employee is making. Remind yourself that your job is to help, not criticize; to support, not disapprove; to encourage change, not to place blame.

Conducting the interview

If this is the employee's first formal interview (and even when it is not) be prepared to reduce the tension, anxiety, and fear which the employee probably is feeling. You can do this by talking about the employee's strengths first, covering each point in some detail.

Explain that the interview is designed to be constructive—that your main interest is the employee's development and growth in the job. Explain, too, that the process is a cooperative one—that is, you don't expect to do all the talking and when you do talk you will be talking *with*, not *at*, the employee.

Next, let the employee talk while you listen. And be sure that you are listening with an open mind. Be willing to learn about the employee. Do not interrupt or cross-examine. Avoid argument. Let the employee bring out both facts and feelings. Perhaps the employee will identify all the areas where improvement is needed and suggest plans for accomplishing necessary change. This could certainly happen if you have been evaluating frequently. But you will never know unless you give the employee a chance to talk.

If the employee does not mention shortcomings or outright failures, and these exist, you will have to discuss them openly—what they are and what can be done about them. Introduce your recommendations for a specific improvement program and let the employee add his or her ideas. Then, together, you should work out a new set of goals.

Some interviews will be particularly difficult, no matter how well prepared you are. It's especially hard to talk with certain kinds of employees—for example, those who are defensive about their work, those whose high opinion of their work does not match up with your evaluation of reality, or those who have unpleasant personalities. In some cases, there is just no hope that both the supervisor and the employee will leave the evaluation interview happy. But don't give up too quickly.

Show you are concerned and interested in your employee's point of view. Keep the discussion focused on job-related issues. Back up any criticism with facts and examples. Be firm if you have critical comments to make. You may be able to prompt positive changes in even your most difficult employees.

End the interview when you have made all the points you intended to make and the employee has done the same. Employees should not be tense or defensive at this point. Their emotions should have been expressed by now, and you should have developed a joint plan of action. Just before the employee leaves reassure him or her that you are interested in his or her progress and also that you are quite willing to discuss it again at any time.

Keeping the employee's record

Whether you are making informal evaluations or formal ones, factual information about the worker's progress should always be written down and placed in the personnel file. No elaborate system of record keeping is required, but all significant facts should be written down (they do not need to be typed), kept up to date, and shared with the employee.

All *actions* should be recorded: goals that are set, job production, specific achievements on the job, action taken by the supervisor to help the employee, and recognition given for accomplishments.

In addition, supervisors should write down *impressions* of how the employee and the supervisor feel about these actions. For example, was it easy or hard for the employee to reach the goals that were set? How did the employee respond to the supervisor's suggestions for improvement or training? How does the supervisor feel about the employee's long-term career interests?

If the employee moves on to another supervisor you should go through the personnel record and take out all the impressions you have written down. Send along the facts about the employee, but omit the guesses and the judgments you have made. Remember that the law protects all individuals against certain violations of their personal privacy (see Chapter 13 for a further discussion of this matter).

Let the new supervisor make his or her own estimate of the worker's ability on the basis of the facts in the file. The new supervisor may have standards that are quite different from yours. Besides, the new job may require a different set of abilities, so that your opinions would be out of place.

While this type of record is kept mainly for supervisory evaluation of the employee, it is important to have these facts recorded for other reasons. For example, if they are not recorded an employee could file a grievance or discrimination suit and the supervisor would be unable to justify a decision made

Reduce tension in the evaluation interview by talking about the employee's strengths first.

months ago. If there is no written evidence of the facts that the decision was based on, the supervisor will not have any defense.

Remember, too, that when the time comes to make a decision or recommendation about an employee (and that time could come with very little advance notice) it is too late for the supervisor to begin collecting information. With good record keeping, all the supervisor has to do is review the file and come to a conclusion based on facts.

And when you consider the many different types of information that must be recorded for different employees in different jobs, you can see that keeping a file of facts is much more useful than trying to use a single rigid, all-purpose performance evaluation system for all employees. You cannot make all employees fit the same evaluation system any more than all police officers will fit into the same size uniform.

Your best approach, then, is to be conscientious about collecting information and flexible about how you use it to evaluate different types of performance in different jobs. To come up with an evaluation system tailor-made for each employee, ask yourself the following questions:

What is the purpose of this evaluation?

What do I need to know to achieve this purpose?

What information do I need to collect to support the evaluation?

At this point you will know what kinds of facts and impressions you need to keep in the employee's personnel file. Then, when it comes time to make an evaluation, ask yourself: Do I have enough of the kind of information I need to make a sound decision about this employee?

Evaluation and compensation

Two questions are often asked about the evaluation of work performance. The first of these is: Should an employee's wage or salary be based solely or largely on his or her performance evaluation? This question causes considerable debate among personnel specialists. Some claim that it is not proper to adjust a person's pay without basing it on evaluation of performance—that those who do more and better work should get greater compensation than those who do less—and perhaps not so well. And they are right.

Many personnel specialists, however, believe that most supervisors do not have control over a sufficient number of factors in the pay area to allow them to make this direct link between what a person does and what is received as pay. They, too, are right—for the compensation area does involve such considerations as the financial conditions of the local government, the amount budgeted for increases, and changes in the cost of living.

This, of course, makes it hard for the supervisor to choose which practice to follow.

The second question is: Should a supervisor's reviews of employee performance be conducted separately from reviews for wage or salary adjustment?

The practical path for dealing with both of these questions seems to be to conduct frequent performance evaluations to give each employee the opportunity to improve performance as he or she goes along. Then at some specific point—perhaps once a year, but separate from the annual evaluation interview—the supervisor should sit down with the employee to discuss wages or salary. All of the aspects that have an effect on compensation should be considered at this time. Within the limits created by all of these factors (including those over which the supervisor has little or no direct control), the supervisor can recommend an adjustment in the employee's pay to reflect his or her overall performance. Obviously, the employee's overall performance is determined by weighing the results of all the performance evaluations since the last compensation adjustment.

Most of the discussions a supervisor has with employees about performance, then, should be developmental in nature—focused on improving performance in the future. Wage or salary adjustments are primarily designed to recognize and reward past performance and to keep the person's rate of pay at a level that is appropriate and fair for the services rendered. When the two evaluation activities are kept separate and distinct, the supervisor and the employee can concentrate on the specific purpose of the discussion.

Remember though that your local government's personnel policies may require these activities to be done in a particular way. Your role in determining compensation may be very broad or very limited.

In some local governments, those with more authority in the work group than the supervisor, such as the supervisor's boss or department head, may conduct evaluations. This may be an especially frustrating situation for the supervisor, and it is important for the supervisor to keep these individuals informed about each employee before evaluations are made.

Legal considerations

Recent court decisions have emphasized the following factors, which should be carefully considered in evaluating an employee's work performance:

Evaluation must be significantly related to important elements of work behavior specifically associated with the employee's job.

Even if the evaluation is clearly based on the best judgments and opinions of the supervisor, it will not be held sufficient unless it also includes definite identifiable criteria based on quality or quantity of work or specific performances supported by some kind of record.

Evaluation cannot be based solely on the supervisor's subjective observations.

Documentary evidence supporting evaluation elements is required.

The evaluation process is full of pitfalls for the biased supervisor. You should make each evaluation as if you were going to justify it to the employee, your boss, a judge, and a jury.

One final point should be made. As has been mentioned before, as a supervisor you will want to help people so that their work will improve. But you should remember this: No one can change another person. The desire and will to change must come from inside that person.

It follows, then, that you should try to create the atmosphere that makes change possible, using methods of working with employees that make it comfortable and even easy for them to change, grow, and develop.

Checklist

Be sure that employees understand their authority, responsibility, and place in the work group.

Let the employee take part in setting his or her goals, standards of performance, and ways of measuring accomplishment.

Compare work results frequently with the goals you have set and agreed on.

Do not evaluate until you have enough of the right kind of information to do a fair and thorough job.

Work with the employee to make the evaluation, devise ways of improving work performance, and set new goals.

Use a formal interview process if a great deal of change in job performance is needed.

Keep written records on all actions and impressions.

Keep performance evaluations separate from salary adjustment evaluations.

DEVELOPING AND MAINTAINING DISCIPLINE

The state of discipline of any group of people depends essentially on the worthiness of its leaders

Henri Fayol

Chapter 13
DEVELOPING AND MAINTAINING DISCIPLINE

What is the purpose of discipline?

How can you prevent disciplinary problems from occurring?

What steps should you take when a discipline problem occurs?

What disciplinary action should be taken?

The supervisor's responsibility is to maintain discipline. This means maintaining efficiency, cooperation, and proper work conduct among employees to achieve desired goals. At the same time, the supervisor is responsible for protecting the rights of all employees in the group or unit.

For this reason, it helps to know that the word *discipline* comes from the word *disciple*—a person who follows the teachings and examples of a respected leader. Like a disciple, the average worker who respects the leader or supervisor follows his or her teachings because they are contributing to meaningful and worthwhile goals. These workers recognize that rules and standards are needed to help everyone get the job done quickly, safely, and well. Discipline does not mean punishment.

Effective supervisors recognize that the average employee wants to do a good job. They help the employee by setting a good example, by matching the right person to the right job, by giving clear instructions, by observing and evaluating everyone's work periodically, and by praising a job well done. They reinforce each employee's self-control and self-respect, and create a well-disciplined and self-disciplined atmosphere.

Unfortunately, not all supervisors employ this positive approach built on mutual respect and self-control. Some supervisors with an old-fashioned outlook practice a negative discipline based on threats of punishment. They believe employees will not obey rules unless they are watched closely and forced to obey. They watch for mistakes and rule violations so that violators can be given the punishment they deserve. They want the employees to know who is boss!

Often such supervisors get the desired behavior from their workers, but usually only when they are looking. Their workers obey rules only to keep out of trouble while the boss is around. Since they fear and dislike their boss, they fear and dislike the rules.

Most employees, however, expect to follow certain rules and regulations that govern their performance on the job, use of equipment and materials, safety and health, and standards of acceptable conduct. Often in a well-disciplined group, if an employee steps out

"Discipline" comes from the word "disciple"—a person who follows the teachings and example of a respected leader.

Developing and maintaining discipline **153**

of line, his or her fellow workers will put pressure on him or her to get back on the track. As a supervisor, you can bolster your employees' desire to do what is expected by helping to strengthen each employee's self-discipline and by avoiding typical causes of discipline problems.

Most causes of troublesome behavior can be traced to one of the following:

Discontent, which comes from boredom, idleness (lack of work), or lack of interest in the work

Ignorance, which comes from lack of instruction, guidance, goals, training, or experience, or a misunderstanding of rules and standards

Belief that one has been treated unfairly

Personal problems that cannot be left at home.

Frequently the supervisor has created situations that produce behavior problems. Without realizing it you may be doing one of the following:

Enforcing rules unfairly or inconsistently

Reinforcing poor job performance by ignoring it

Rewarding poor conduct by giving it more attention than good work

Rewarding good work with additional work, thereby overloading the good worker.

Your relationship with your workers is a powerful force for developing commitment to organization rules. Let us look at some of the steps you can take to build mutual respect and appreciation.

Strengthening self-discipline

Step 1: issue clear, reasonable rules and regulations

Begin by reviewing all the rules and regulations that apply to your department and work unit. You should be thoroughly familiar with them. Be sure that each one is needed to create an orderly, efficient, and safe work environment.

If you feel a rule is unfair or poorly written you should recommend to your supervisor and your department head that it be reviewed and changed. Make suggestions on how to improve it. Be sure, too, that all rules can be enforced consistently. If a rule cannot be applied to everyone it should not be made or enforced.

Finally, be sure that standards for job performance are set so that the average employee can attain them.

Step 2: set a good example

To keep morale and discipline high, you should expect good performance from everyone, especially yourself. Demand good work and good conduct from yourself, so that you can ask for the best from others. Get to work on time. Keep on schedule. Meet performance standards. Submit reports on time.

A supervisor must be self-disciplined and present a good role model as a leader to be able to discipline others effectively.

Step 3: communicate clearly

Each employee should know what is expected. Employees should know what work should be done, at what quality level, when it should be finished, and why it is being done. They should also know what acceptable standards of work and of behavior are.

When an employee is hired he or she should be told what the policies and rules of the department are, what the penalties are for breaking the rules, and how these penalties can be appealed.

There are several methods supervisors can use to call attention to the rules and to ensure that employees understand them. Any or all of the following may work for your own group:

Give each employee a copy of the employee handbook, if there is one, which contains personnel rules and regulations and other applicable rules for the working group.

Post the rules and regulations on a bulletin board for easy access.

Help the worker understand how his or her job fits in with the whole work group.

Have the person in charge of training conduct an orientation program for new workers.

Conduct a series of meetings with employees to explain the rules and to help employees understand them—especially those employees who have reading difficulties; encourage employees to make suggestions and ask questions at these meetings, and be sure that they have ample time to do so.

In talking to employees about the rules and procedures in your department, you should use simple, clear language and give specific examples. Remember, too, to tell workers about those regulations that are especially important to your own department and work group—the ones that will be enforced strictly.

Pressure from fellow employees will often bring a worker who has stepped out of line back on the track.

When discussing penalties for breaking rules, explain clearly which violations result in severe penalties such as dismissal, demotion, suspension, or reduction in salary.

Supervisors often forget to give information about job standards. The employee should know from the beginning how much work is expected, and what its quality should be.

Hold meetings at regular intervals to review standing rules and regulations, and pass along information about new policies or rule changes.

Careful, patient job training can give employees the skills they need to do a good job. You may want to use procedure manuals, training programs, films, and other aids. Above all, you will need to devote extra time to coaching and encouraging new workers while they are learning.

Step 4: keep complete records on workers

As a supervisor, you have the responsibility of keeping records of each person's work and of the work of your unit as a whole. This kind of record keeping is useful to top management and to you in planning and evaluating your work load. It is also an important step in establishing a positive discipline program.

These work records should contain each worker's responsibilities and duties, job goals, and major accomplishments, as well as copies of letters of commendation, and records of training courses attended, leave taken, and disciplinary action taken, if any. You may want to furnish a new employee immediately with copies of some of the records going into his or her file.

In keeping this type of personnel information or working files on your employees, you should remember that the law protects all individuals against certain violations of their personal privacy. And interest in protecting the informational privacy of individuals is increasing. For example, in recent years many privacy bills have been introduced in the U.S. Congress and in state legislatures.

It is important, then, that the information you keep in your working files is information that should be there—information that has to do with the job and the employee's performance and behavior on the job. If, for example, you hear from someone that one of your employees is having an extramarital affair, that is (1) hearsay and (2) purely personal information and does not belong in the file on that employee. It does not relate to the job and it may not be true.

In addition, you should be careful as to who can see your files or can have information from those files. The best rule to follow is: Does the person have a legal right to know? Any information relating to an employee's job or performance or behavior on the job should be available to your superiors or any other individuals in the local government who really need to have such information to do their jobs.

It is a good idea to allow the employee to see the information in his or her own file that relates to performance appraisals, records of awards or letters of commendation, formal disciplinary actions, work assignments, production records, and the like. Then if any information is wrong it can be corrected. But such information as your own notes about an employee's work and work behavior you will probably want to keep to yourself. You also have a right to privacy.

Do not give any information contained in your working files to anyone from outside your local government, or to those in the local government who you feel do not really need the information—unless you are told to do so by the personnel officer or by higher management. If this is not the case, however, and someone should call you on the telephone, the best course is to tell the caller to contact the personnel officer or the chief administrative officer of your local government. In this way you are protecting the privacy of the employee and also protecting yourself.

Note that disciplinary action is *only one small part* of the contents of this file. Be sure your employees understand that their work records are not intended as records of their mistakes and rule violations but are balanced accounts of their accomplishments on the job. These records should be open to employees and they should be encouraged to look at the materials regularly.

If and when disciplinary problems do come up, then the work record will help you decide how to handle them in light of the past performance, both good and bad, of employees. It should be borne in mind, however, that if work records are to be used as evidence when employees are being penalized for an offense, the supervisor must be able to show that a record has been kept on *all* employees, not just on one or two problem employees.

Dealing with rule violations

Let us assume that you have built a good relationship with your workers. You have strengthened their desire to do a good job. You have given them clear instructions and have been generous in praising a job well done. Your workers are self-disciplined, productive, and satisfied.

But sooner or later, despite your good efforts, an employee will break a rule or fail to meet the standards that have been set. You will then have the unpleasant but necessary task of dealing with that employee to correct the situation.

When disciplinary action is needed the supervisor must strike a balance between ig-

noring rule violations altogether and pouncing on every mistake. The disciplinary action taken by the supervisor should be aimed at guiding the employee, strengthening the employee's self-discipline, and improving the employee's work behavior. The penalty the supervisor chooses should be the mildest penalty that will accomplish these changes.

Let us look now at the steps that should be taken by the supervisor when a rule has been violated.

Step 1: act promptly

When a violation occurs, do something about it immediately. This does not mean that you should reprimand or punish the worker on the spot. It does mean that you should immediately make notes on all important details of the incident.

You should immediately try to find out exactly what happened, and you should be sure that the person who violated the rule knows you are looking into the matter. If you do or say nothing when a rule is broken you are condoning the violation. When workers see that you are not enforcing a rule, they soon stop abiding by it and it ceases to exist for all practical purposes.

Step 2: get all the facts

Most disputes about rule violations arise over the facts. This is why supervisors should re-

member that the most important thing to do when a rule has been broken is to *get all the essential facts, and then write them down.*

You should gather all facts as quickly as possible for the following reasons:

The details will be forgotten if there is a delay.

You need facts to decide if a rule has been broken.

You need facts to decide who broke the rule.

You need facts to decide what action to take.

You need facts so that your decision making will be objective.

You need facts if your disciplinary action is challenged by a worker who has been penalized.

The facts you gather should give a complete word picture of the situation so that anyone reading them can feel that he or she has been a witness.

Informal memos are often a good way of setting forth the facts. Whatever form your report takes, it should answer the following questions:

For a rule violation: (1) get the facts promptly; (2) get the facts in writing.

Who was involved?

Exactly what happened?

When and where did it happen?

Who else was there or nearby?

What did you say to the employee?

What did the employee answer?

Be sure to ask the employee for an explanation of the incident and record the answer. Do not decide whether the explanation is true until you have investigated it thoroughly. If no explanation is given, this fact could be important, especially if an explanation is made at a later date at a grievance hearing. Pass no judgment until all the facts are in hand and you have had time to review them.

Step 3: decide what action to take

When you have gathered all the facts you can, have spoken to everyone concerned, and are convinced that the employee did violate a rule, you must use your best judgment to decide what to do.

Take the time you need to make a proper decision, but do not delay too long. Consider all relevant factors and get all the advice you can. You should consult your supervisor and the personnel office at this point. They can help you to be sure that you are following local government policies and legal requirements and that the action you take is not stricter or more lenient than the action that would be taken by other supervisors.

To decide what penalty is necessary (if any), you should first decide how serious the offense was. You will want to ask yourself the following questions:

Why did the worker commit the violation?

Was it a major offense?

How much trouble did it cause?

How many people or dollars were involved?

Was one rule broken? More than one?

Has the employee a good conduct record?

Has the employee a good work record?

How long has the employee worked in the department?

When was the last disciplinary action (if any) taken against the employee?

Did the employee understand the possible consequences of the violation?

Keep in mind that the purpose of disciplinary action is *to change an employee's behavior*—not to "get even" with or to humiliate the employee. How a supervisor deals with a disciplinary problem is a question of circumstances, precedent, the supervisor's judgment, and the employee's personality. Strict discipline with an ordinarily stubborn or rebellious employee would probably produce different results than with one of a more compliant nature. Any action you take should be constructive. It should bring about compliance with the rules.

When you are making your decision consider the possible effects—both good and bad—that your action can have on this employee and on other employees. And whatever action you decide to take or to recommend to your supervisor, you must be prepared to explain it and defend it with facts.

There are two approaches to disciplining employees. Some believe that penalties create feelings of anger and the desire for revenge, and that they actually produce negative behavior in a worker. Workers who fail to meet standards or obey regulations are told what the consequences of their problem behavior are and are told what they must do to improve their conduct. (Of course, workers who commit crimes or such serious offenses as fighting, intentionally damaging property, or frequently getting drunk on the job might be fired or otherwise strongly disciplined as soon as all the facts are known.)

A second approach is to penalize workers who break rules or fail to meet standards, with the idea that penalties will change their behavior.

Usually there is a range of penalties—from mild to severe—which supervisors can use. Following is a discussion of disciplinary actions in common use. Usually, the appropriate penalty is the least severe penalty that is at the same time strong enough to convince the employee that the behavior that brought about the disciplinary action will not be tolerated. As the penalties become more severe, it is important to document prior problems and the use of a progressive sequence in the discipline used.

An *informal talk* is usually given to employees with good records who have broken a minor rule. They are told that they have violated a rule and are asked for an explanation. They are cautioned about repeating the violation, and the matter ends there. No record is kept of this kind of action.

A *spoken warning* is somewhat more severe. In this case the employee is told that his or her behavior must improve or more serious action will be taken. This warning should always be given in private. A record of the warning should be placed in the employee's work file, but not in his or her permanent record in the central office. If the employee's behavior improves, the report of the warning should be removed from the file after a certain period of time, usually six months.

The *written warning* is similar to the spoken warning but is more severe. It is used for more serious offenses or for employees who have broken the same rule several times.

The written warning should mention any prior warnings given; should describe what the employee has done wrong; should indicate what improvement is expected and the time limit during which the improvement should be made; should state what will happen if improvement is not made; and should offer the supervisor's help in bringing about a change in conduct.

The employee keeps a copy of the warning. Copies are also placed in his or her permanent record as well as in the department's work file. The warning can be removed from these files after a period of time if the offense is not repeated.

Suspension is a far more severe penalty. An employee who is suspended is removed from his or her job—usually from one to thirty days—without pay. This serious disciplinary action is usually subject to review by top management. You will almost certainly need the approval of your superior and the personnel office for such action.

Suspension is used when a major rule is violated or continual warnings have not succeeded in bringing about changes.

The employee must be interviewed before suspension is decided on. He or she is then notified in a letter delivered personally by the supervisor or by certified mail. The letter should state the reasons for the suspension and the dates on which it begins and ends. It should also tell the employee how, to whom, and by what date he or she can appeal the action.

Salary reduction is another severe penalty. An employee's salary may be reduced when suspension has been tried but the problem behavior has continued. The employee must be notified in a letter stating the reasons for the action and spelling out the exact amount of the reduction. The employee's right of appeal should be explained.

Demotion is another severe form of penalty. Demoting an employee to a lower job level is unlikely to improve his or her attitude and may actually make it worse. For this reason demotion is used rarely as a form of discipline, or is used merely as a last resort before dismissal. Usually a demotion can be authorized only by a department head or the local government's top management.

(In some cases employees are placed in lower job levels because they are having difficulties coping with their jobs. Then the demotion is not a disciplinary action and should not be treated as punishment.)

Dismissal from the job is the most severe penalty of all—the ultimate penalty. It is, of course, reserved for the most serious offenses, and used only after everything else has failed. In many cases only your department head or the government's top management can authorize dismissal, after sufficient time has been taken to gather all the facts so as to ensure that the penalty is justified.

Transfer, while it is not a disciplinary action, is sometimes resorted to as a method of solving a problem of employee conduct. Transferring a problem employee to another department or work group is valid only when there is a personality conflict between employee and supervisor that keeps both from working efficiently and affects the morale of the whole unit. It should be emphasized that transfer is inappropriate as a disciplinary action and should not be used as one. Arranging to remove a troublemaker from a particular work group is not a way of solving a problem. It simply passes the problem on to another supervisor.

Step 4: hold a disciplinary interview

Suppose you have gathered all the facts about a rule violation and have considered all appropriate disciplinary actions. Before you make the final decision you must talk to the employee who violated the rule. The purpose of this interview is to get his or her side of the story, beyond a factual recounting.

The interview should be conducted in private, without interruptions by others in the office or by the telephone. Encourage the employee to talk. Listen carefully to his or her explanation and look for the reasons underlying the employee's actions.

Have all of your facts organized and at hand, and have your questions ready. End the discussion when the employee has been heard in full and when there seem to be no new facts to add.

At this point you should tell the employee what he or she did wrong and what disciplinary action you have decided to take or to recommend to your superior. You should have a good idea of what action seems appropriate when you begin your interview, and you should change your mind only if the employee gives you some valid *facts* which you had not considered or did not know about beforehand. You should not change your mind because the interview makes you feel more or less sympathetic toward the employee.

You should also agree on what the employee must do, and in what specific period of time, to improve his or her behavior. You should be sure that the employee knows what changes are expected, and when, and what will happen if no changes are made.

Finally, before the employee leaves, you should inform the employee of his or her right to appeal your decision and you should explain how, when, and where the appeal can be made.

Be calm, neutral, and fair, but firm and businesslike throughout the interview. If you find you are losing your temper, interrupt the interview and reschedule it for later in the day. Treat the employee like the adult he or she is and restrict your comments to the employee's behavior; you should not criticize him or her as a person.

After the interview is over, you should write up the main points discussed. Be sure to include the goals for improvement that were agreed upon. The record of the interview should be kept in the employee's work file.

Step 5: use the appeal procedure

Under our legal system an accused person cannot be judged by the person who accuses him. But in your position you are both accuser and judge when it comes to disciplining employees. The possibility of wrongly accusing a person is great in this kind of situation and must be guarded against.

This is why in a good disciplinary system the employee is given the right to appeal to a third person. As supervisor you should inform the employee about the procedure for appealing, and help him or her with the appeal if necessary.

Typically, the procedure for appealing a disciplinary decision is clearly stated in the local government's personnel policies. If you are not familiar with the procedure, you should contact your department head or the local government's personnel office to determine the steps in the process and how to assist the employee in making the appeal. In many local governments someone in the personnel office is assigned the responsibility of assisting the employee.

As the employee's supervisor you should emphasize to the employee that he or she has complete freedom from reprisal if his or her choice is to appeal the disciplinary decision. Remember, if an employee feels wronged and cannot get justice inside the organization, he or she may decide to take you to court outside the organization—a situation that could be most unpleasant for all concerned.

Special considerations in unionized local governments

Discipline is one of the most common problems for supervisors in local governments that have bargaining units. The supervisor has a responsibility to discipline employees fairly based on the labor contract procedures, and a labor contract always modifies disciplinary procedures. Most of the points already discussed in this chapter are applicable to union-represented employees; in addition, usually these employees will have a right guaranteed by contract to appeal your disciplinary decision a final step to a neutral third party.

The most severe form of discipline, dismissal, is always discussed in the labor contract. Most contracts state that dismissal can be only "for cause" or "for just cause." The legal effect is to require that the constitutional guarantee of due process as defined by state and federal court decisions be observed in any dismissal action. If you dismiss an employee in a unionized local government, a step-by-step process should be followed before that employee is deprived of his or her job or income.

Decide what has happened and write a letter or a memorandum to the employee explaining your concerns. Include factual allegations in writing and cite the employer rules that were violated. ("Allegation" is a legal term for a statement you intend to prove.)

Give the employee a copy of any written complaint upon which a disciplinary action may be based.

Let the employee know in writing about any disciplinary action you are considering, such as suspension or discharge.

Give the employee a chance to reply to the allegations in writing. Show a specific date and time for his or her reply, and allow at least forty-eight hours from the time of receipt of your allegations.

Give the employee a chance to talk to you personally and present his or her side of the story. Set up a definite date, time, and place for the meeting, usually one day after the employee's written reply.

Let the employee know in writing when the decision will be made and when it will be made known to the employee.

Allow the employee to resign, but do not suggest or urge the employee to resign, or offer any incentive for the employee to do so.

It is always prudent to check with your superior, the personnel office, or the labor relations office to review the steps to be followed for dismissal or other major actions. In addition to being good management practice, this assures a defensible position if your action is appealed.

Checklist

Know the personnel rules and regulations of your organization.

Establish fair work standards.

Brief your employees on the rules and regulations of the local government, the department, and the work group.

Have a regular method for discussing changes in policies and rules with employees.

Maintain a file on all employees in your work group.

Set a good example by following all rules yourself.

Apply rules consistently to employees.

When a disciplinary situation arises try to get all available facts.

When you have to correct an employee's behavior, discuss the problem privately.

Direct your comments toward the problem, not the person.

Let the employee tell his or her side of the story during the disciplinary interview.

Always end the disciplinary interview by telling the employee what, if any, disciplinary action you have taken or have recommended to your superior.

Inform the employee of his or her right to appeal, and safeguard that right.

Avoid making an example of the disciplined employee to other members of the work force.

Be consistent in applying penalties on the basis of the severity of the offense.

Always check with your superior and the personnel office or top management, as necessary, before implementing any severe disciplinary action.

RESOLVING EMPLOYEE COMPLAINTS AND GRIEVANCES

14

The search in the settling of disputes should always be for the best future activities of the parties concerned

Mary Parker Follett

Chapter 14
RESOLVING EMPLOYEE COMPLAINTS AND GRIEVANCES

What is an employee grievance?

What are the causes of grievances?

How can you recognize potential grievances?

What steps should you take in resolving employee grievances?

Wherever people work you can expect to hear complaints. Handling employee complaints requires patience, tact, understanding, and sound judgment. But above all it requires a procedure for airing and resolving complaints and an effective supervisor who can make the procedure work.

Supervisors who develop skills in handling complaints build good relations with their workers, improve employee morale, and can improve the operating efficiency of their work unit, thereby contributing to their local government as well.

Every gripe that is ignored and allowed to become a formal grievance is costly. You pay for it in low production, absenteeism, high turnover, and loss of support from the community around you.

As gripes, complaints, and grievances are a normal part of living and working, let us take a closer look at what they are, what causes them, how they can be prevented, and how they can be resolved.

Your local government's personnel policies may establish the process you must follow. If your workers are covered by a union-negotiated contract, the contract may require a particular procedure. In either case, as a supervisor you have a major role, perhaps the most important role, in handling complaints and grievances. Indeed, your ability to handle them may determine how effective a supervisor you really are.

Gripes, complaints, and grievances

When we talk about griping we are talking about the kind of complaining people do simply to let off steam. People who gripe usually do not expect a change and may not even want one. It is their way of relieving the strain of living with a situation that they know they cannot change. The man who gripes about the traffic jam on the way to work and the woman who gripes about the food in the cafeteria are using words to help make the best of situations they dislike.

The next level of dissatisfaction—the complaint—is more serious because it does require that a change be made. Complaints fre-quently involve relatively minor matters at work that can be settled on the spot. If an employee complains, for example, that his equipment still has not been fixed, or that the new employee working with him still does not know how to do his job, a phone call or some reassuring words might well take care of the matter.

Both gripes and complaints can grow and become formal grievances if they are not handled satisfactorily. If a gripe or complaint becomes a formal grievance, there must be a step-by-step process for resolving it. A formal grievance is a written expression of an employee's dissatisfaction with some part of the job or working relations with others on the job that he or she cannot control. Usually, the basis for a formal grievance is clearly stated in the local government's personnel policies, and the grievance is about a local government policy, rule, regulation, or the like.

It is important that every supervisor make sure that the conditions of employment agreed to by the organization are carried out fairly and honestly—that practice coincides with promises and policies.

However, it is equally important that management's rights (your rights) not be encroached upon by the employee. Grievances are not allowed on management issues. For example, management has the right to determine the following:

Organizational structure to be utilized

Work to be performed

How work is to be performed

Tools, machines, and equipment to be used (except when a safety hazard is involved)

Money to be spent in performing the work

Selection of supervisory personnel

Standard of selection of employees.

Often employees can make constructive suggestions on the above issues and supervisors should always listen attentively, but a grievance cannot be filed on these subjects.

A grievance grows out of an employee's feeling that he or she has been treated harshly or unfairly by the organization, by fellow employees, or by the supervisor. If employees think they have been wronged (even if it is a misunderstanding) they express their frustrations and resentments in the form of grievances.

When employees have actually been wronged by someone or something, there is a real grievance. Such grievances are usually easy to resolve because the facts are clear and an appropriate change or adjustment can usually be made.

Employees can also have imagined grievances, which may grow out of misunderstandings, rumors, or wrong information. In some cases setting the employee straight will take care of the matter. In other cases the supervisor has to deal with a real issue behind the imagined grievance.

An employee may insist, for example, that the computer makes an error on his paycheck every week. If this turns out not to be true, the supervisor may find that the real problem is that the employee is not getting the salary he expected.

The supervisor's first job is to decide whether the employee is merely griping or complaining, or is voicing a legitimate grievance. If it is a grievance, is it real or imagined? Temporary or permanent? Something that can be resolved or something that is an unchangeable part of the job? Is it a problem that the supervisor can solve? Or is it a grievance that should be settled by top management? Or does it involve an issue where management rights take precedence and a grievance cannot be filed?

The causes of grievances

In some cases grievances voiced on the job may be reactions to something that is happening in the employee's private life. A person who is unhappy at home often finds reasons to complain in the office. But the kind of grievance we are going to discuss here is

a formal complaint that grows out of a situation at work. Let us look at some of the situations that cause grievances.

Work assignments

Workers are often dissatisfied if they have more ability than their jobs demand, or if they have less ability, time, or training than is needed to do their jobs properly.

Employees who are already working as hard as they can may feel frustrated if they are assigned rush jobs or overtime by a supervisor who has not given any thought to distributing the work load evenly.

Working conditions

Excessive noise or dirt, poor lighting or ventilation, dangerous equipment, and shortages of tools or supplies are examples of poor working conditions that may become sources of grievances. On the other hand, grievances can grow out of relations with people as well as things. Dissatisfaction can grow out of the nature of the job itself, out of problems with co-workers, or out of difficulties with you, the supervisor.

Relations with the supervisor

Most employees want to like and to get along with the supervisor. When they do not, the reason can be a misunderstanding, or a personality clash. At other times, however, it is the supervisor's mistakes that lead to complaints and grievances. Workers are often dissatisfied if supervisors have been guilty of the following:

Failing to set forth clear job policies

Failing to plan work properly

Giving too much or too little supervision

Setting unreasonably high or low work standards

Failing to listen to employees

Failing to delegate work authority to employees

Failing to keep employees informed

Allowing rumors to go unchecked

Criticizing an employee in front of others

Using sarcasm or ridicule instead of constructive and task-oriented criticism

Being inconsistent or unfair in enforcing rules.

Personal problems

Employees, like supervisors, bring their whole personalities—including their per-sonal problems—to work with them each day. Personal problems stemming from the home environment can emerge in the guise of grievances. It is the supervisor's responsibility to be able to distinguish a problem that began at home from a real work grievance. In the case of the former, the employee may need counseling or other personal help. How to deal with this kind of problem is the subject of Chapter 11.

It is obvious, then, that as a supervisor you have to know your workers as individuals. Call them by name, get to know something about their families and personal interests, and keep an interest in their lives outside of working hours.

Recognizing and preventing grievances

Recognizing a grievance is not difficult. When a problem has reached such proportions the worker with the grievance will probably be making the matter obvious. That is the purpose of a grievance—to call attention to what an employee feels is an unfair situation. It is more difficult to recognize a gripe or complaint that could develop into a grievance.

The causes and prevention of grievances.

The supervisor who wants to keep trouble from developing should watch for danger signals. Grievances may first show up as a change in employee behavior, especially a change from good to bad habits, attitudes, or work habits. Happy workers may become moody and gloomy. Sociable people may begin to keep to themselves. Enthusiastic workers may begin coming to work late and may appear to drag through the day. Careful workers may become careless daydreamers.

Sometimes the danger signal is a flare-up. A worker may refuse to follow orders, or may tell you off. In short, you should suspect some dissatisfaction when any of the following danger signals appear:

Lack of enthusiasm or cheerfulness

Excessive griping about the local government, the department, or the work group

Lack of interest in the work

Excessive tardiness or loafing

Too many errors

Reluctance to assume responsibility

Decline in output

Excessive short-term sickness.

Through preventive measures an effective supervisor should catch problems when they are small and easier to deal with. And when you correct unsatisfactory conditions before they get out of hand, your workers will feel (and rightly) that you are interested in them.

Some of the important ingredients of a "preventive maintenance" program are: talking frequently with employees, providing an outlet for complaints, observing employees, keeping track of working conditions, showing appreciation, and helping employees get ahead.

Talking frequently with employees

Be approachable. Keep employees posted on what top management is doing. Do not let them get all their information from the grapevine. When they have the facts they will understand why things are done in a particular way and will be more likely to cooperate with management policies.

Put all policies and practices in writing so that all employees know what to expect from the organization and what the organization expects from them.

Develop a genuine interest in your workers, their interests, families, and problems away from work. Of course, a balance should be struck between your interest and concern and what may strike employees as prying.

The message to convey is that you are available for advice and referral and that you have a genuine interest in them as individuals. This type of effort certainly pays off in fewer gripes and fewer complaints.

Providing an outlet for complaints

It is important to create an atmosphere in which employees feel they can express their complaints without fear of punishment. Such an atmosphere provides a safety valve for letting off steam. Remember that employees have a *right* to voice grievances, and they should feel free to tell you about their complaints. And it is far better for them to complain to you than to fellow employees, or not to complain at all. The effective supervisor, then, not only provides opportunities for workers to blow off steam but *encourages* them to do so.

These supervisors are aware of something else: by talking with a sympathetic and understanding listener, a person can gain valuable insights into a personal problem. Employees may begin to understand and solve their own problems when they have a chance to tell them to someone.

Effective supervisors also know that grievances are not personal criticisms. They listen carefully and show by their actions that (1) they are concerned about their workers' problems, (2) they will try to do something about the complaints brought to them, and (3) bringing up complaints will never have any bad effect upon an employee's relationship with the supervisor—or with anyone else in the organization.

Observing employees and working conditions

You should be sensitive to changes and danger signals in employees' moods and work habits. Are they getting the work done? Are they working well with others? Do they need more training? Are they interested in what they are doing? If not, what can be done?

An employee cannot put in a good day's work without proper tools, supplies, equipment, protective clothing, and cooperation from other workers. And no one functions well in a work area that is stuffy, dark, or dirty. Do not wait until workers complain about working conditions. Check these conditions continually to see if they can be improved or if any changes need to be made.

Even when a supervisor does not hear any complaints, he or she should not assume that everyone is happy and satisfied. It could be that there is no procedure for handling complaints, the procedure is not working well, or the employees lack confidence in the supervisor. Whatever the reason, it is up to the supervisor to help open up the lines of communication by encouraging workers to speak out.

Failure to consult with employees on matters directly affecting their jobs is a primary cause of grievances.

Showing appreciation

No one likes to be taken for granted. If an employee does something that deserves recognition, let that employee know you appreciate it. A word of appreciation will do a lot toward building morale and satisfaction with the job.

Helping employees get ahead

If you think employees have the ability to qualify for promotion, tell them how to do it and encourage them to try. This can be one of the best ways of raising morale and increasing job satisfaction. It can also help to eliminate griping.

Systems for handling grievances

Sooner or later the day will come when you are faced with a grievance that you were unable to foresee or prevent. How are such situations handled?

There are many different systems set up to help employees air and settle their grievances. In unionized organizations, formal procedures are usually set up and employees and supervisors are required to follow these procedures step by step, whenever a grievance is filed.

The procedures in nonunionized local governments are sometimes as formal as those in unionized organizations. Whether procedures are formal or informal, the objective of these systems is the same: to make sure that employee grievances can be heard, and to make sure employees can seek relief without fear of penalties as a result of expressing their feelings.

Systems for handling grievances should contain the following elements. They should:

Protect an employee's basic rights as a citizen

Fit the size, complexity, and operating conditions of the organization

---

Be simple and easily understood by employees

Allow the employee to be accompanied or represented by an individual of the employee's choice

---

Be written out and brought to the attention of all employees

Provide a prompt, satisfactory response

Be fully understood and supported by all levels of management.

The last point is especially important. Unless all managers above the supervisor believe the grievance system is important and are committed to making it work, the system will fail regardless of how well it is designed.

Most formal grievance systems specify a number of steps an employee can follow. Almost all of them require that the grievance be put in writing and reported to the supervisor first. If at all possible, a grievance should be settled at this point.

Procedure for handling grievances

Once an employee presents you with a grievance, in person or in writing, and you have decided that you are the proper person to hear it, you must decide what to do about it. No matter what the formal procedure is in your organization, you can probably get best results by following these suggestions:

Determine responsibility for trying to settle the grievance.

Listen attentively as the grievance is presented.

Question the employee to gather a full set of facts.

Get additional facts and verify statements made by the employee.

Keep adequate records to show that the grievance has been investigated thoroughly.

Analyze your alternatives.

Decide who has the authority to act.

Make your decision promptly.

Explain your decision to the employee.

Follow up your decision.

Here are some techniques you can use to carry out these recommendations for handling grievances.

Accept responsibility

To decide whether you should consider an employee's grievance personally or refer it to someone else, ask yourself the following questions:

Does the employee work for me or for someone else?

What is the local government's procedure and policy?

Am I responsible for correcting the situation?

As an employee's immediate supervisor, you have a responsibility to try to resolve the grievance. You are in the best position to get information about the problem and you

Suggested steps in processing employee grievances.

can act more promptly than anyone else. You should not pass the buck unless the problem is clearly someone else's responsibility. (But keep in mind that if the employee is not satisfied with the solution you propose, he or she may appeal the decision and have it reviewed by managers at higher levels.)

Nor should you ignore a complaint because it seems trivial to you. Remember, many serious grievances had their beginnings as small complaints.

Listen attentively

How you listen may have a lot to do with how easy it is to settle the grievance. Always bring employees with grievances into your office if you have one or some other private place. Put them at ease. Let them know they are welcome and that you are interested in what they have to say.

Demonstrate your interest by listening calmly and carefully to the employee's story from beginning to end. Listen with an open mind and attentive attitude. Do not show emotion—especially disapproval or disbelief. Do not argue or cross-examine. And always keep your temper, even if the employee does not.

Try to see the situation from the employee's point of view. Taking a grievance to a supervisor is often a nerve-racking experience. It means taking the initiative with a superior and doing it in a situation that might be very controversial. The employee knows that his or her position represents only one point of view.

Now try to understand that point of view and the reasons behind it. If the grievance turns out to be unfounded, treat it as though it were real because it *is* real in the employee's mind. Calmly ask the employee to repeat the story. It is very important that you understand every word. Also the first telling may not reveal what is really bothering the employee, while the second telling often gets at the underlying causes of the trouble. Take a few notes to help you keep the facts straight and to assure the employee that you are taking the grievance seriously.

Question the employee

Take your time to get a full set of facts; remember, when an employee submits a grievance to you, you are being asked to correct a situation or an action. You cannot decide whether or not to do either one unless you have a complete picture of the situation. Facts will decide the case. And when the employee sees that you will not act before you get all the facts, he or she is less likely to misrepresent them.

At this point you should remember that the employee has given you a set of facts designed to support his or her case and to get a settlement in his or her favor. Ask yourself if there are any other facts in the situation. Ask yourself if there are any facts that do not support the employee's case.

To find out you should ask some basic who, what, where, why, and how questions about the case. Try to phrase the questions so as to get more than a simple yes or no answer. When these answers are in, state the grievance in your own words and ask the employee whether your statement of the problem is correct. Until you and the employee can agree on a statement of the problem you do not have a common understanding of what the grievance is about.

Then tell the employee you plan to gather more information about the problem from other sources and that you will discuss the matter with him or her again when this has been done. If possible, give the employee some idea of when you will do this.

Do not, at this point, make any statements at all about the merit of the grievance, especially not statements that would lead the employee to think you have taken sides in the matter.

Get additional facts and verify statements

In any grievance procedure you must base your decision on facts, not personal opinions or statements that have not been checked. It is important that you verify information given to you by the employee and gather more information. Check records and reports; get other people's observations and ideas; and talk to witnesses, others who know about the case, and people who have been through similar experiences. Other critical matters to check are: any policies of your local government that may have been violated; any departmental policies and practices that may apply to the case; any previous grievance settlements that may provide a precedent.

Many situations may exist in the local government that you are not familiar with. Consult your supervisor, other supervisors, and staff specialists such as the personnel officer to get advice or to get more information. A technical opinion from an expert is often helpful as well. You might want to ask a mechanic, for example, whether the brakes on a fire truck involved in a grievance were in good working order.

Keep adequate records

You should take notes throughout the grievance procedure. And it is especially important to keep a written record of the employee's statements that you have been able to verify and of the facts that you get from other people. Be especially careful to keep a record of basic facts such as names, dates, and times.

Keep your written records; they will be needed by the next management level if your decision on the grievance is appealed. In fact, do not discard written records of any grievance procedure—even those that were settled to everyone's satisfaction.

Analyze your alternatives

When you have all the information you need in writing, put the facts together in an orderly way and list the decisions that you could reach in the case. Test each alternative by thinking about the impact it might have on the employee, on other employees in your work group, and on the organization as a whole. More specifically, ask yourself these questions about each of your alternatives:

Is it fair?

Will it solve the underlying problem?

Does the solution conform to city policy, rules, and regulations?

Is it consistent with past actions taken?

Does it establish a good precedent?

If you answer no to any of these questions, or if you are not sure of the answer, check with your superior to get suggestions.

Decide who has the authority to act

Before you choose one of the alternatives for action, be sure that you have the authority to act. Many grievances involve laws, ordinances, budgets, local government policies, or other factors over which you have no control. You may have to consult with your own supervisor or the personnel office to get the advice or support you need if you have any doubts about your authority to settle a grievance. You should also check to see if your organization has a formal grievance procedure that tells you what to do if you are unable to settle a grievance yourself. Grievances involving suspensions, salary reductions, demotions and dismissals are likely to be difficult to resolve and in many cases will be appealed to your department head, local government manager, personnel board or local elected council. If you do not have the authority to make a decision (or if the employee decides to appeal), pass all the facts to the next level, which in most cases will be the department head.

Make your decision promptly

Putting off decisions is a human thing to do, but it gives employees with grievances the impression that you are against them, and that the settlement—even if it is a satisfactory one—is made grudgingly. A speedy decision is especially important in settling grievances that involve an employee's health and safety. Such grievances often bring out strong emotions in employees and should be resolved as soon as possible. Be sure to put your decision in writing.

Explain your decision

Explain carefully and calmly what the written decision is, how it was reached, and why it was made that way. Be clear and straightforward. If action is to be taken by the organization explain what will be done and by what date.

If the fault was yours, admit it. Do not put the blame on someone else. Your honesty will encourage employees to admit any mistakes they themselves may have made.

Ask the employee if the decision is acceptable. If it is not, be sure the employee understands that an appeal may be filed. Review with the employee the procedure for appealing the decision. Let the employee know you are glad he or she came to you with the grievance. Tell the employee that you bear him or her no grudge, and encourage the employee to come back if new facts are found or if he or she wishes to discuss the problem further.

When your talk with the employee is over, write down what was said and what was decided. Keep this written record along with all the other records of the grievance procedure.

Follow up your decision

Be sure to live up to your commitments and check to see that others involved in the decision live up to theirs. If action was referred to someone else, find out whether the matter was actually settled.

Some time after the decision has been explained to the employee get in touch with him or her again to report any new developments, to indicate that you are still interested in the employee, and to find out whether the grievance has actually been resolved from the employee's point of view.

Special considerations in unionized local governments

In unionized local governments, the grievance procedure is one of the most important parts of the year-round administration of the labor contract. You should be familiar with the contract grievance definitions, procedures, and timetable to assure full compliance with the contract. Many supervisors and managers do not understand the importance of careful and consistent handling of grievances. Remember that grievance decisions set precedents and these precedents are as binding as the labor contract. Be sure you know the limits of your authority to settle grievances under the labor contract.

While grievances should be resolved promptly, they should not be handled hastily under union pressure. Also, you should not hesitate to get help from the personnel or labor relations offices about personnel rules or contract provisions.

You should never be casual, humorous, or hostile in conducting grievance proceedings. If an employee or union steward feels a matter is important enough to appeal formally under the contract procedure, your sensitivity to the personal feelings of the employee as well as the legal considerations will help in successfully resolving the matter.

Finally, you should understand that a contract grievance is often not a matter of who is right or wrong but of what works best for both sides. Approaching grievance disputes with rigid attitudes usually works against successful problem solving. Willingness on the part of the supervisor and employee to "mediate" voluntarily can help create a satisfactory result for all. This will require technical knowledge, proper authority, and thought from you to bring about successful resolution of a grievance. Remember, every settled grievance is a legal precedent and may affect the outcome of the next grievance that comes up.

Checklist

Know your employees: their work, their problems, and their interests.

Watch for situations that cause grievances.

Correct such situations before a grievance is filed.

Give an employee a good grievance hearing; listen attentively and seriously without interrupting.

When the employee has finished stating his or her case, ask questions, but take no position.

Ask the employee to repeat his or her story, then repeat the essentials in your own words.

Take notes and keep records on the hearing.

Get all the facts available.

Check departmental policy and practices.

Seek advice if necessary.

Check previous grievance settlements for precedents.

Check the experience of others in similar cases.

Make a proper settlement as quickly as possible.

Explain your written position to the employee.

Once a decision is made, stick to it unless new facts come to light.

Pass all the facts to the next level if you do not have the necessary authority to make a decision or if the employee decides to appeal your decision.

Take the corrective action required by your decision.

Follow up to make sure that action has been carried out.

CONTROLLING WORK PLACE LOSSES

Supervision and safety go hand in hand

National Safety Council

Chapter 15
CONTROLLING WORK PLACE LOSSES

Why is loss control important to you and to your employees?

How do accidents happen?

How can you learn from near misses?

Where can you get help?

We pay a high price when employees, property, or other resources of the city or county are lost to the work force. Whether the loss is due to accident, illness, fire, theft, vandalism, or absenteeism, everyone pays! Monies spent for repairs or replacements or liability payments or training new employees are not available for delivering services to citizens, increasing pay for employees, or upgrading facilities and equipment. The price we pay in dollars and in emotional stress is especially unfortunate because it is so unnecessary. In times of tight money when we have to do more with less, loss control is a vital part of every supervisor's job.

What can and should the supervisor do to control losses? Where does the supervisor fit into a comprehensive safety management program? What are the consequences of an accident for the supervisor, the employees, and the organization? This chapter tries to answer those questions.

Are safety programs really necessary?

Think about it. What happens if a worker is injured or even killed at work? First, the worker and his or her family suffer physical pain and emotional upset. The worker loses income (workers' compensation insurance provides only partial income). The loss of regular pay strains the family's budget when it may already be struggling with medical bills.

The cost of an accident to the city or county can be very high—even if no one is injured. There may be higher insurance premiums; damage to buildings, equipment, tools, or vehicles; service delays. Perhaps time will be lost as new workers are trained, the work load is rescheduled, the accident is investigated, and reports are completed.

What causes accidents?

Although we know that people do not plan or intend to "have an accident," accidents are *caused*, they don't just happen! Fortunately the causes can be determined and controlled.

It helps to understand what the sources of accidents are, and to think of these specifically in *your* work place. There are four sources, which can interact to cause an accident.

The first source of accidents is *people*, all employees in an organization. Motivation,

training, and performance evaluation (covered in chapters 8, 10, and 12) play a big role in preventing accidents. Employees must have the know-how and the willingness to work safely! *Equipment* is the second source. This includes everything from vehicles to hammers. Using faulty equipment or adapting it to perform tasks for which it isn't designed can lead to accidents. *Materials* that employees use can contribute to accidents. They may be sharp, heavy, hot or toxic! Finally, there is the *environment*, which includes the buildings employees work in as well as the air they breathe.

When there is an accident, the supervisor should consider each of the four sources in determining the cause.

An update of H.W. Heinrich's domino explanation of accidents illustrates how accidents happen and shows what supervisors can do to prevent accidents.

Lack of control by management

The first domino in the sequence of events that leads to loss is lack of "control" by management. Something you can do as a supervisor to maintain proper control is to make sure there is proper orientation and training, and that rules are established and followed. Inspecting worksites and equipment, holding safety meetings, and investigating all accidents are also important. Almost without exception, the first domino will fall for the

The employee is not the only loser in an accident.

supervisor who does not plan and organize the work, and who doesn't motivate and lead employees to the proper level of performance.

Basic causes

Lack of management control permits underlying or basic causes of accidents to exist. Basic causes can be divided into two groups:

Personal factors that cause poor performance include lack of knowledge or skill, poor motivation, and physical and mental problems. Job factors are inadequate work standards, inadequate maintenance or design of equipment or materials, normal wear and tear, and abnormal usage. If a supervisor fails to recognize and change or correct these basic causes of accidents the second domino falls.

Immediate causes

When the basic causes exist, they set the stage for unsafe practices and conditions.

Unsafe practices include operating without authority, operating at improper speed, using defective equipment, using equipment improperly, failing to use personal safety equipment, horseplay, and drinking and drug abuse.

Unsafe conditions can be inadequate guards or protection, defective tools or equipment, inadequate warning systems, fire and explosive hazards, substandard housekeeping, hazardous conditions (fumes, noise, etc.), and congestion.

These are only *symptoms* of the basic causes, but failure to remedy them means failing to keep the third domino from falling.

The accident

When unsafe practices or conditions are allowed to exist then an accident or a near-accident is usually the result. An employee may trip or fall; be struck by something; be caught between or against or under something; or be electrocuted, burned or poisoned. The fourth domino has fallen.

The loss

Once the entire sequence has taken place and there is an accident, whether to people or property, the resulting loss is usually determined by chance. It can be a minor, a major or a catastrophic loss to people or to the city or county government. But long before that last domino falls there are many things a wise supervisor can do.

Supervising with safety in mind

Accidents are most easily prevented at the point where the work is done—that's why, even if your government has a safety coordinator, you as a supervisor play a key role.

But you cannot prevent accidents single-handedly. You will need the help of top management to provide proper conditions and facilitate proper practices. You will need the help of your employees to design a safety program and cooperate to make it successful.

Making employees safety conscious

Helping employees to be safety conscious is a good start in preventing accidents and controlling losses. Safety precautions are often thought of as unnecessary nuisances even when they involve very little effort. (Think of how many thousands of people are killed in car accidents each year because they do not want to take two seconds to snap a seat belt closed.) Successful teaching always involves setting a good example. If the supervisor shows dedication to a loss control program by his or her daily actions, employees will tend to follow the lead. Example is more effective than lecturing or scolding.

Discussions are another way of focusing attention on safety. Whether they are with individual employees or groups, formal or informal, the important thing is to encourage employees to do the talking. Help them to think about their own behavior and its effect—about what is safe or dangerous.

Often it is easier for employees to talk about specific incidents or problems than about the large, vague topic of safety. You might ask them questions to get them started: What are they doing that is safe? What are they doing that is dangerous? Why did a certain accident occur?

Discuss details as much as possible. Try to get everyone's ideas on what caused a particular accident. By the end of the discussion everyone should have contributed something and the entire group should agree on how this type of accident can be avoided in the future.

In addition to discussion, you might demonstrate some safety techniques—how to lift heavy objects, for example—and then allow members of the group to practice. But no matter how you focus attention on safety, keep your meetings lively and worthwhile. If they are a routine chore for you they will be dull for those who attend.

Think topics out in advance and be well prepared, so that no one's time will be wasted. Choose topics that are current and timely—how to use a new piece of equipment, or how to behave in a specific emergency. Try using some of the visual aids and other training ideas available from the sources listed later in this chapter.

Above all, remember that people will be committed to loss control only if they have a voice in pinpointing the problems and suggesting the solutions. An effective way to involve employees is to form a loss control committee that will meet on a regular basis.

When the supervisor is gazing at the horizon . . .
when no one is paying attention to job methods . . .
when one bad habit leads to another . . .
when employees are not working as a team . . .
accidents are bound to happen.

This committee can be made up of a cross section of employees representing different levels and types of work. The committee can: review accidents and determine whether they were preventable or unpreventable; conduct on-site inspections at the work place for hazards; and develop a safety awards program. An awards program can spark interest and awareness among employees. Awards themselves can be anything from recognition and a personal letter to a cash bonus. Several different events throughout the year keep safety and loss control in the minds of employees.

Reporting

One of the most important things you can do is to ensure that *all* accidents are reported. This includes those accidents that don't involve injury. Near misses can be significant!

Keeping records of the type of accidents that occur in your work unit can help you spot trends that demand special attention. Accident reports will help you pinpoint training needs, modify work procedures, and eliminate special hazards on the job. Equally important, the documentation is essential for worker compensation claims.

Learning from near accidents

Often when there is a near accident we breathe a sigh of relief, count our blessings,

Be sure all accidents are reported. Serious injuries are only one part of the total loss picture.

and go on about business as usual. What we need to do is take advantage of those close calls to look for underlying *causes*. As you can see from the compilation below, made in a study of almost two million accidents, for every accident in which serious injury occurs there are several hundred near accidents. If we only investigate serious accidents, we may be missing the boat.

1	serious injury
10	minor injury
30	property damage
600	no visible injury or damage (near accidents)

You have probably heard or read that the Federal Aviation Administration investigates near misses. The lucky pilots are alive and well and can report what *almost* happened. If the FAA waited to investigate only accidents, it would not get many first-hand reports of what *did* happen. Investigating the near miss leads to improved procedures and elimination of particularly dangerous situations or work routines, so that a real accident is prevented.

Being prepared

You can prepare for emergencies. Knowing first aid and having a plan for getting prompt emergency care could save an employee's life. It's too important to leave to chance!

Getting help

There are many sources of help available to you in controlling losses. Some of these are listed below:

The insurance company or state agency that handles your workers' compensation can provide posters, films, and other safety training materials, as well as accident report forms and advice on safety engineering.

The department of industrial safety in your state has experts in all fields of engineering—mechanical, electrical, and

If you don't watch for danger points,
you won't find them.

mining engineering, for example—who can usually help you solve your safety problems.

Many private businesses have experts on their payroll who can help you with specific problems.

Many local health departments (state and federal agencies, too) have a variety of information available for local government use. Most public health departments will act very quickly if a supervisor reports an occupational health hazard or a contagious disease.

The National Safety Council has many services for members (your city might want to join), including bulletins, posters, and safety training aids. The public employees section of the council publishes a newsletter devoted exclusively to safety problems (and solutions) in government operations.

Professional and trade associations such as the American Public Works Association and the American Water Works Association can also provide information and assistance in safety matters.

Don't overlook the sources in your own organization. Employees who work in fire prevention, in emergency medical services, those who are in inspection and police investigation, all have special skills that can be very helpful.

Avoiding pitfalls

A common error to avoid is leaving the identification and solution of problems to management alone. Employees resent a safety program imposed from above and often resist it. They may disregard the program, report sick, or do careless work. Whatever form it takes, employee resistance wastes time and money—and does not bring about a safer work environment. Remember to involve your employees in planning and implementing a safety program.

Another common error is looking for physical causes of accidents or other losses while overlooking the attitudes and feelings of workers, which are frequently to blame. For example, some workers who dislike their jobs will work carelessly (without realizing it) as a way of striking back at management. Any resentment or stress in work or personal life can lead to loss or accident on the job.

Finally, it is well to be aware that poorly planned safety programs can actually increase accidents by arousing hostility in employees. When workers feel that safety policies are inconvenient, unnecessary, or inappropriate, or that they do not work well, they will not use the safety equipment, will ignore the safety rules, and may express their resentment by doing something careless that causes an accident.

Again, a way of avoiding these mistakes is to use the workers' knowledge of their jobs

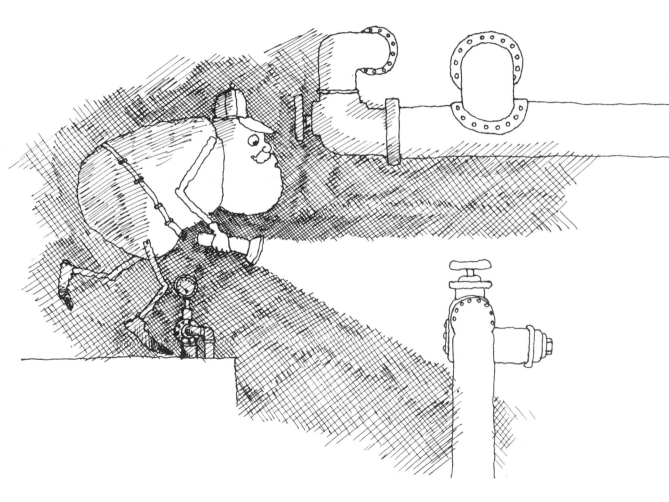

All too often, job safety is limited to visual inspection of our immediate job surroundings.

and their interest in working safely as a team. If they have a meaningful part in creating the program they will be far more likely to support it.

Checklist

Remember that your attitude toward safety and loss control sets an example for all workers.

Be sure that you have the support of top management in getting the money, worker time, and policy changes needed to provide safe conditions and encourage safe practices.

Remember that safety planning must be by and for the workers. You cannot plan a safety program alone and expect it to work.

Remember that workers must be safety conscious if accidents and losses are to be prevented: you will need to stir up and maintain interest in a safety program.

Remember the domino sequence and *learn* from accidents and near accidents. Don't just *count* them!

Remember that a little prevention may save a lot of pain.

WORKING WITH THE BUDGET

16

Where thrift is in its place,
and prudence is in its place,
. . . there the great city stands

Walt Whitman

Chapter 16
WORKING WITH THE BUDGET

Why does my department have to spend so much time on the budget every year?

What is the difference between the capital budget and the operating budget?

What is my responsibility in budget planning?

How can I get the money I need to meet my work goals?

This chapter provides information, guidelines, and strategies to help you, the supervisor, understand your local government's budget, the process used in preparing it, your role and responsibilities, and how you can manage your part of the process better.

Functions of a budget

Your local government, by law, must prepare a budget every year. From start to finish, the process will take three to six months, endless departmental meetings, council work sessions, and public hearings. Yet, in the final analysis, this year's budget may look pretty much like last year's—making you ask yourself, "What's all the fuss over the budget anyway?"

The fuss over the budget, and the reason it takes so long to develop, is that a local government budget is much more than just account codes and dollar figures. The budget serves three very different functions: control, management, and planning. Some people use the budget only for control, and others only for management; still others are interested in all three purposes. Confused? Let's briefly look at each function of the budget.

Control

First and foremost, your local government budget is a legal document. Once it is approved by your elected officials, you and other government officials are bound by law to adhere to it. Therefore, you should spend only the money specified in the budget for your department unless approval to do otherwise is given by elected officials. Your expenditures will be carefully watched to assure that you spend funds in accordance with the purposes described in the adopted budget. Therefore, if your budget calls for you to buy a new police car, you cannot decide to buy new uniforms instead. The control purpose of the budget casts a somewhat negative tone on the budget, but you should not think of it in this way. Instead, remember that you are spending public tax dollars on programs for the citizens in your community and therefore you should be held financially accountable for your actions.

Management

As a management tool the budget is a way of stating what your local government plans to accomplish during the coming year. Your responsibility is to make sure you find the most efficient way of providing a service, given the money you have to work with. For example, you may determine that the least costly way for the parks and recreation department to operate is to maintain large parks with municipal crews and hire private contractors to maintain small traffic medians.

Planning

As a planning tool the budget reflects the major program and policy objectives set by your elected officials for the coming year. Many times elected officials become frustrated when they realize how little of the budget they can control. Salaries, benefits, pension fund obligations, debt payments, street maintenance expenditures, and other fixed costs necessary to maintain your local government leave little room for elected officials to cut taxes, begin new programs, or increase expenditures for pet projects.

The budget shows how your community elects to spend its tax money, a limited resource; some programs receive more money this year while others receive less. For example, your elected officials may decide they want to spend money for a large number of recreation programs to keep adolescents off the streets rather than spend more money to have the police keep them out of trouble. This particular objective or "plan" would be shown in the budget by an increase in the number of dollars spent by the recreation department, and a hold on the dollars for the police department. The council is using the budget for planning and for deciding how money should be spent. As a supervisor, it is your responsibility to carry out these plans.

Who uses the budget?

The budget is not only a local government document, but also a public document. It is used by local government officials and citizens alike. Below is a review of the different people who will use the budget during the year.

Elected officials

As mentioned above, elected officials use the budget for planning, in order to set general policy for the community. The budget reflects their wishes as to what programs and services should be provided and how much money should be spent on these activities. During the course of the year the council may frequently refer to the budget to make sure programs are being carried out according to its directions.

Management

The chief administrator and department heads use the budget to manage and control. They want to make sure that you are doing your job in the most efficient way. They will be checking to see that you stay within the budget approved for your section by the elected officials.

Citizens

First and foremost, citizens are interested in the bottom line of the budget, that is, how the total budget has changed since last year and what effect the change will have on their tax rates. The budget should assure them that their tax dollars are being used wisely.

Citizens look at individual programs and services listed in the budget to find ways to save tax dollars. For example, they may suggest that the refuse department change from backyard to curbside trash pickup to save money. They may also propose changes to the budget if they want elected officials to increase or decrease the level or quality of a particular service.

Interest groups

These groups may be the "Northwest Neighborhood for Safer Streets," "Mothers for Day Care," or any other group interested in a specific program or activity in the budget. Generally, an interest group will want more money spent on this program or activity. It will usually be the elected officials who have to deal with these groups. Interest groups will also watch you and your department, however, to make sure you are delivering services in the best possible way.

Business groups

Business groups, such as the downtown merchants, take both a broad and a narrow view of the budget. Since they are usually major taxpayers in the community, they want to know how the budget's bottom line will affect tax rates. They will also be interested in specific services, such as road maintenance or police protection, that are important to their businesses.

You, the supervisor

The budget is your authority to operate. It is the most important guideline you have for your operations, and the budget is used to hold you accountable for the money you spend. The budget will lay out what services and programs you are responsible for and the money you can spend on them. How you actually accomplish these tasks is up to you. If you need to spend more money than was approved in the budget, it is usually necessary to get approval from management. If the change is significant enough, your elected officials may have to approve it through a budget revision action.

Types of budgets

Nearly all local governments have two separate budgets: an operating budget, which includes revenue estimates for the year and planned expenditures for all ongoing government activities, and the capital budget, which includes revenue sources and planned expenditures for all equipment and facilities to be purchased that year. Frequently these two budgets are combined in a single budget document, but they should be considered by

The budget lays out the component costs to finish the project and shows you how much money you will have to spend.

you and your elected officials separately. Below is a discussion of each type of budget.

Operating budget

The operating budget is the local government's plan for allocating resources (tax dollars and other revenues) for personnel, supplies, equipment, and the operation of facilities needed to provide services to citizens and run the other activities of the government. There are several kinds of operating budget formats used by city and county governments. You should check with your department head or budget officer to see what budget format you will be working with as a supervisor. The most usual ones are line-item, program, and performance budgets, and less frequently, the zero-base budget. A brief description of each follows.

The line-item format organizes a budget by categories of expenses for each department, division, or agency within the local government. There are generally two broad expenditure categories in the line-item budget: "Salaries" and "Other expenses." Under "Salaries," department heads and supervisors distinguish between regular salaries, part-time, overtime, and so forth. In the "Other expenses" category, there will be separate amounts for contractual services, materials and supplies (gasoline, pads, pencils, utilities, tools), and equipment (two-way radios, repair parts). Many local governments use a line-item budget because it provides a clear explanation of what will be pur-

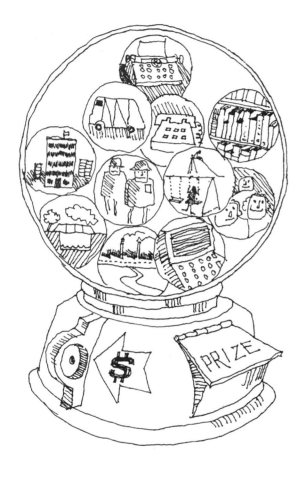

Expenditures are not a random process but rather are planned for specific targets.

chased with tax revenues. It is designed primarily to prevent overspending, and provides strong central control over departmental expenditures and aids elected officials in comparing the new budget with prior ones. The line-item budget is widely used by smaller local governments.

The program format organizes a budget by major activities, such as trash collection, street sweeping, vehicle repair, crime investigation, and summer athletics. Many local governments that budget by program also include some line-item detail in order to identify and control the cost factors (personnel, supplies) in each program. A program budget is used by many medium-size and large local governments.

The performance format organizes a budget by the work to be accomplished in each program (building inspection, street maintenance, tax collection) and the cost to do it. For example, a performance budget will list the number of miles of streets to be swept in a year and the cost per mile. A performance budget is similar to a program budget in that it organizes the budget by activity. However the performance budget goes a step further, by also listing and pricing the *amount* of work to be accomplished in each program. Partly because of the additional record keeping it requires, the performance format is not widely used by local governments.

A zero-base budget (ZBB) is organized like a program budget, but during the budget

process elected officials consider a variety of funding levels for each program and then select the level they believe best meets the needs of citizens, given tax dollars available. For example, a public works department may list three levels for street sweeping: low level—sweep each residential street at least once per year; moderate level—sweep each residential street three times per year; high level—sweep each residential street monthly. The advantages, disadvantages, and cost of performing an activity at each level of service are also included. Each level of service for each program is ranked by the department head. Elected officials may then give their own rankings to levels of any service according to their priorities. Resources are given first to those programs that are of highest priority to the local government. While a ZBB calls for the preparation of alternative budgets for all programs in order to determine the advantages and disadvantages for each, only one of the alternatives is chosen to be included in the overall local government budget adopted for the year. ZBB is used by a small number of local governments.

Capital budget

Before reviewing the capital budget we need to briefly discuss a related document, the capital improvement program (CIP). The CIP is a multiyear plan for making major purchases of equipment or facilities, such as: a new wing for city hall, a library, a new road, sewers, heavy equipment, or data-processing equipment. It would not include items such as typewriters, supplies, or anything used or "consumed" in the day-to-day operations of the local government. Capital items, therefore, are different from other government purchases in that they are generally more costly and nonrecurring in nature. The CIP also proposes the means for financing capital items.

The capital budget is published with the operating budget and explains the spending plan for the first year of the CIP. Financing for the capital budget may come from local government tax revenues, a state or federal grant, or long-term borrowing. The capital budget is usually not a separate budget as such, but is included as a section of your government's operating budget. It may be shown in different ways. There may be a few pages at the beginning or end of your operating budget summarizing the capital budget expenditures for the year. Or each department's operating budget may include its capital budget request as one of the line-item or program categories. Or capital expenses may be shown both ways. In any case, remember that the operating portion of the budget shows recurring, day-to-day expenses while the capital portion of the budget shows major, usually one-time purchases of equipment or facilities.

While capital improvement programming and budgeting is an important planning device many small local governments may not have a capital program or a capital budget. Generally these jurisdictions have an item or items in their regular operating budget called "capital outlay," where items of a capital nature are listed.

The advantages of a capital improvement program are:

It can reduce major fluctuations in tax rates by scheduling and financing the costs of capital facilities over a number of years.

It encourages the coordination of capital and operating expenditures, so that the impact of capital projects on the operating budget can be anticipated. For example, the building of a new library, a capital expense, will affect the operating budget since the local government will have to staff and maintain the new facility.

It allows flexibility in scheduling bond issues, which may result in more favorable rates when the local government borrows money.

It helps coordinate capital projects with state and federal aid programs. Urban renewal grants, for example, require that a municipality have a capital program.

A capital program is a good public relations tool in that it helps the taxpayer understand the community's long-range needs and what is being done to meet them.

It can assist in pinpointing the reasons for a tax increase and show whether the increase is related to operating costs, capital costs, or both.

Other local budgets

Some local governments require other budgets in addition to their annual operating and capital budgets. They are almost always for a specific purpose or the operation of a specific facility. Some of these other budgets depend on federal aid programs and therefore are not fully integrated into either the operating or capital budget. Some arise out of special financing arrangements whereby fees or even some taxes are paid directly to municipal agencies and are dedicated to the support of a particular service. Water and sewer systems, electric utilities, and housing programs are often operated in this way. Generally, each separate fund will require a separate budget.

The budget document

After many hours of work by you and your department head, and review by citizens and elected officials, the operating budget is adopted. As a legal public document the budget is available for all to see. Here is what it will include:

The budget message

This is usually submitted by the mayor or chief administrator to communicate to the council, the citizens, and the media the major elements of the budgets, including total projected expenditures for the year, any new taxes or increases in taxes, new programs and activities, and an overall analysis of the local government's financial health.

Revenue estimates

This is a statement of the estimated revenues (and their sources) necessary to fund the operations of the government. Frequently, information from the one or two preceding years will be included so that increases or decreases in revenues can be seen. An explanation of any new revenue sources may also be given.

Program expenditures

This will show where money is being spent and for what purposes. Your activity's budget may or may not be separately shown depending on the type of budget your local government uses (e.g., program, performance, or line-item).

Work statements

These are either general or specific statements of what your local government will accomplish during the coming year. For ex-ample, 210 miles of street will be swept monthly (public works); 16 girls' softball teams will be organized (recreation); 160 inquiries at the library will be answered each month (libraries). If your budget includes work statements they will be integrated with the section on program expenditures so that it is apparent how much each particular activity costs.

The budget process and your role in it

In all likelihood you will work closely with your department head in organizing your budget. However, it is important that you learn how to prepare and present a well-thought-out budget request. The better you are able to develop and present your budget to superiors (and ultimately to elected officials), the more likely it is that your request will be approved. Below are the five primary steps in the budget process and your role in each step.

Step 1: budget planning

The preparation of a budget begins three to five months prior to the beginning of your local government's fiscal year. During this period the people responsible for the overall budget prepare estimates of revenues for the coming year based on tax projections, anticipated state and federal grants, and estimates of fees and charges and other miscellaneous revenues. If you are responsible for a service for which a fee is charged (e.g., inspections, recreation programs), you may be asked for information to help prepare the revenue estimates.

Step 2: departmental budget preparation

Usually four months before the new fiscal year, supervisors and their department heads will prepare their individual budgets.

Generally, budget forms, instructions, and work sheets required for preparing the budget will be provided by the budget staff. If you have never used these forms before, you will need to review them carefully so that you understand exactly what is required. Before completing the budget forms, you and your department head will consider the work and activities your unit will be involved in for the coming year.

You may plan to repeat past years' activities or you may propose to add, subtract, or change some activities. For example, as the supervisor of a recreation center you may feel that you need to offer more programs for senior citizens because the composition of your neighborhood has changed. Or, as the supervisor of a police shift, you may be aware that elected officials want to increase police patrols in the center of town during evening hours. You will have to factor this possible increase in service into your budget request. Each activity of your unit should be translated into work load data (number of new senior citizen programs, frequency of patrols needed). The key to work load data is that it must be credible and understandable. It will be the basis for your budget request.

Once you establish your work load for the year you will calculate the personnel, equipment, material, and other costs needed to complete it. For example, if five major snow storms per year are typical for your area and the council wants all primary streets cleared within twenty-four hours, you should determine the number of miles of road involved and the number of miles each snowplow can clear per hour. You can then calculate and justify the need for specific levels of personnel and equipment. Your department head or the budget staff can assist you in calculating personnel, supply, and equipment costs.

In preparing your budget request there are three guidelines you should remember:

Keep the budget simple. Use simple language and basic terms that can be easily understood and explained. Everyone viewing your budget needs to understand the terms you use. Don't assume that all people understand abbreviations or understand why you need to purchase a certain commodity. Your goal is to promote understanding of your particular budget. Informed decisions by local officials regarding the budget will result in a more cost-efficient government.

Provide enough detail so that citizens and elected officials can understand what is being requested and why. For example, data on the miles of streets to be maintained, the number of inspections, the types of inspections, etc., provides the detail needed. In justifying salaries and wages, show the number of hours worked, hourly rates, and numbers of people occupying part-time and full-time positions. Show the position titles rather than individual names whenever possible. Don't assume this year's budget should be the same budget as last year's, "plus a little more." If a budget request is reduced by elected officials and the proper budget detail has been provided, spending reductions will be related to service reductions, such as reducing the number of inspections, or number of recreation programs offered.

Separate the capital items from the operating expenses. Capital items are those used for more than one year, usually three or more years. Any capital equipment request should describe which items are replacements and which are new. The age of existing equipment should be shown as well as the original cost. The need for any new equipment should be explained and related to a new or expanded service whenever possible. If a new vehicle is needed, then include a thorough explanation of the need as well as the trade-in value of the old vehicle.

Once the departmental budgets have been prepared, they will be organized into the

preliminary local government budget by those people who coordinate the overall budget. At this stage in the budget process estimated expenditures usually exceed projected revenues. Since revenues must equal expenditures in a balanced budget, some adjustments will be necessary.

Step 3: internal budget review

At this step the chief administrator and other key persons will review budget requests with department heads and prepare a balanced budget to send to elected officials. Very likely many changes will be made during this stage. Requests which seem high will be cut back. If your department head cannot explain your budget request, it may be sent back to you for more details. You may be asked if you can do the same work with less staff, or if you can find less costly ways of performing a task. At the conclusion of the internal budget review the budget will be very close to being in balance and can then be sent on to elected officials for consideration.

Step 4: external budget review

During this step elected officials will review the budget and hold public hearings so that citizens have an opportunity to comment. Elected officials and the chief administrator will also hold a number of work sessions to reshape the budget according to the needs of citizens. Both sides of the budget, revenue and expenditure, will be reviewed, and either may be changed. If the proposed budget requires increased revenue, and elected officials do not want to raise taxes, both revenue projections and expenditures may be lowered by a similar amount to keep the budget balanced. Elected officials may make these cuts themselves or they may ask the chief administrator and department heads to propose budget reductions.

This process will result in the final local government budget, which, when approved by elected officials, is a legal document.

Step 5: implementation

Once the budget has been passed it is up to department heads and supervisors to carry out programs and activities within the funding restrictions of the approved budget. As a supervisor you will want to let your staff know how the new budget will affect them. Will any positions be cut, added, or left unfilled? How will the work change—will employees be doing more of one activity and less of another? Can they expect any new equipment during the year or will they have to make do with what they have? Did elected officials have any specific criticism or praise for the work they have done? It is up to you to see that your employees know and understand the new budget. You may be able to do this yourself or you may need to have your department head do it since he or she will have a broader understanding of the overall budget. In any case, give it to them straight,

"All we need is a basic bridge . . . but you know what inflation has done to the dollar!"

"I want nothing but the best . . . but you know we don't have that kind of money!"

without judging the rightness or wrongness of the decisions that were made.

During the year you need to make sure you stay within your approved budget. To help you monitor your budget you will likely receive a monthly or quarterly budget report showing how much your unit has spent so far this year. Chances are that your department head has already reviewed it, but you should probably review the report briefly just in case an error has been made in staff or supplies charged to your account. If you have been spending funds more rapidly than was expected, your department head will probably want to know why.

Unforeseen circumstances may require that your budget be changed. For example, if a tornado or hurricane strikes your community, the public works department may have to spend many hours of overtime clearing downed trees. Or, if tax receipts are much lower than expected, you may be required to cut your budget by a certain percentage. Your department head will usually work with you if your budget needs to be changed. It will be your responsibility to determine what effect budget changes will have on your activities and staffing levels.

Step 6: planning for next year

What can you do to make the budget process go more smoothly next year? Here are some tips:

Prepare early. During the year keep track of changes you want to make in your activities for the next year. Will these changes have an impact on your budget? Is there a new piece of equipment that will allow you to operate more efficiently? Think about how you will propose desired changes during the next budget process.

Keep track of changes in your work load. Are some activities taking more or less time? If so, why? Try to keep track of these changes and let your department head know about them. This will make it easier to justify changes in your budget and activities next year.

Identify ways in which your unit can become more efficient. Listen to your employees. They may be able to suggest new ways of doing things that can save money. If you think of these things during the year it will be much easier to prepare your next budget, especially if you are asked to do the same work with less money.

Talk with other supervisors. Have they identified new ways to prepare for the budget process? What techniques are they using to stretch every dollar?

Practice. You will be doing a budget every year, so don't fight it. Think about new ways of doing it better. Talk with your department head about your ideas. The budget process is the one time of the year when your activities will be looked at and evaluated very closely. Take advantage of this by presenting yourself, your employees, and your work in the best possible way.

The politics of the budget process (or why your budget was changed)

Once you have completed your portion of the budget, many people will review and change it so that the final version may look quite different from the one you initially recommended to your department head. Your department head may change your budget request before submitting it to the chief administrator or budget staff; it may be changed by elected officials during budget work sessions; it may be changed based on comments from citizens. The question is, why has your budget been changed? After all, you are closest to the work and know what is needed to accomplish it. Here are some reasons why your budget request may have been changed:

You asked for more money than was necessary, figuring your budget would be cut anyway. Your department head realized that your budget was inflated and would never pass the scrutiny of the budget director, city manager, and elected officials. So your department head lowered your budget.

Your budget requests were not clear. Someone, the council, the manager, or the citizens, could not understand the justifications for your budget requests. They weren't sure what you planned to do differently this year that required more staff, or extra supplies and equipment. In a nutshell, your budget wasn't defensible. In most cases your department head will be asked to defend your budget to those responsible for the overall budget. If he or she doesn't have the right answers, be prepared to see your budget changed.

Money is tight. There is never enough money to do everything that needs to be done. Even if your budget is 100 percent accurate, and justified, it may be reduced along with others to balance the overall budget.

Priorities have changed. Last year the elected officials thought it was important to keep streets extra clean so the street-sweeping budget was increased. This year it is more important for the police department to purchase motor scooters to patrol the parks, so the police budget is increased while others are decreased.

The process of developing the budget wasn't a good one. When elected officials are overwhelmed by the budget, they sometimes make cuts or changes just to demonstrate that they have had some say in the budget process. Elected officials need to have confidence that the details underlying the budget are based on sound analysis. In order for elected officials to be effective, budget materials must permit them to understand the local government's overall financial condition, revenue potential for the coming year, and options for meeting the service needs of the community. It is up to the senior management officials to see that elected officials feel comfortable with the budget process and the information they receive.

Bad luck. You think your street repair crew is one of the best in the city, but council members heard that they finish their work forty-five minutes early every day so they figure you need fewer people.

Good luck. Sometimes your budget will be increased. Usually this occurs when elected officials want to see a new service added or service levels improved. This means that during the coming year you will have to provide the new or improved service level requested, and be able to demonstrate that you have done so.

Remember, the budget is a tool used to control, manage, and plan how tax money should be spent. Elected officials and management depend on you for accurate information to formulate the budget, and they depend on your effective supervision to provide citizens with the highest level of service possible with the money available.

Checklist

Think of your budget as your operating guide.

Learn how to do your part in your local government's budget process.

Start collecting information for your budget request early in the year.

Remember that your budget request will be looked at by your department head, top management, elected officials, and citizens.

Promote understanding of your budget request by detailing the costs of services provided.

Keep your employees informed about budget decisions.

WORKING WITH THE PUBLIC

*Where council members,
the mayor, and the chief
administrator are proud of
their city, this feeling
will spread*

David S. Arnold

Chapter 17
WORKING WITH THE PUBLIC

What does it mean to work with the public?

What should you know about your local government?

What should you know about yourself?

How do you handle questions and complaints?

How do you keep informed on the work of your local government?

What is your job in working with the people who live in your community? One way to find out is to ask people what they think about their local government. You might get answers like these:

"I think they do a pretty good job of running this county. Went down to the courthouse the other day to pay my taxes and had no trouble finding the right office or filling out the forms. They've got some real nice, helpful people down there, and everything seems to be organized to make things fast. . . ."

"I don't think they know or care what they do at city hall. The other day they blocked off my street for three hours to fill in potholes and never even let me know. And that was the day I had to park two blocks away

and go back and forth to bring six bags of groceries into the house. . . ."

"I don't know about the rest of the city government, but we sure have a good police department. Do you know they came out and patrolled our street the whole time we were on vacation? And they showed us how to keep burglars out before we left. This is a great town to live in."

Is this a fair way to size up a government? Perhaps not, but people do it that way. Their attitudes about government are based on their own experiences with the people they see doing the work of the government—city and county employees. Right or wrong, you and your fellow workers represent your city or county whenever you deal with a citizen or an out-of-town visitor.

People today demand that business, industry, schools, and government have good leadership, good management, and good services. And they will hold all of these institutions accountable. People today will not support or cooperate with a government agency that fails to deliver services promptly, efficiently, and courteously.

You and public relations

What does all of this have to do with you as a supervisor? It means that you have more influence than you think on people's opinions. You and your employees are doing things

every hour of the working day that affect the way people feel about your city or county government. Your job is to see that the impressions made are good impressions—the kind that win friends and create public support for what you and your government are trying to accomplish. This is a major part of what many people call public relations.

A good public opinion of you, your fellow workers, and your local government has to be *earned*. Do not confuse it with publicity, which means tooting your own horn—*telling* other people what a good job you are doing.

Public relations starts with providing good service. Your department should always be looking for better and less expensive ways of getting the job done. It should also be trying to prevent problems if at all possible.

For example, the fire department helps people learn how to prevent fires and to recognize fire hazards. The building inspector's office advises people on how to construct a safe, strong home or office building. The recreation department encourages physical fitness. The police department gives tips on ways to prevent burglaries. Is there a preventive or educational service *your* department can provide to reduce its work load and improve the health, safety, or well-being of the people in your city or county?

Public relations is a job for everybody—the mayor, the switchboard operator, the maintenance worker, the fire chief, the secretary.

Every employee represents the local government; to some people he or she is the local government.

It is not something you can delegate to a public relations director or public information officer. Every city or county employee represents the local government to the people. This is true both on the job and off. Many people in your community may never meet the mayor or the major department heads, but their impression of local government will be created by you and other employees—the traffic officer who investigates their fender-bender, the refuse collector who empties their garbage cans, or the receptionist who directs them to the right office.

The public consists of people, each person different from others. Keep in mind that many people wear several different hats and belong to several groups. When you try to find out what the public thinks of your department—and you should be doing this on a regular basis—it may be easier to find ways to get this kind of information if you examine your relationship with these groups.

The following list of groups is by no means complete, but it should help you get started in making a list of your own.

Taxpayers: homeowners, business operators

Visitors: from other cities and states

Public officials: city officials, county officials, state and federal officials

Students and teachers: elementary schools, high schools, colleges

Community organizations: chamber of commerce, civic associations, service clubs, lodges, veterans groups

Churches: all faiths and denominations

Communications media: local and area newspapers, radio, television, specialized magazines.

It is a common mistake on the part of government officials to assume that newspaper coverage, because it is extensive and informative, will reach all segments of the community. A similar mistake is to assume that a diversified governmental reporting program—an annual report, tax leaflets, informational fliers, and frequent newspaper announcements—will reach all segments of the community.

Some people can't read; some people won't read. You and others in your local government can best reach these hard-to-reach people by serving them well. Let people you serve know that they are important to you. Think about their personal convenience (as well as yours) when you plan your work schedule. When you and your associates serve all people well, you will be sending a positive message to all people in your community.

Practice timing and courtesy by letting people know when work must be done and by being courteous at all times with all people:

Building inspectors should not expect a friendly welcome if they knock on a door unannounced. Owners of homes or businesses should be notified a few days in advance and given a choice of dates and times if they are to be visited by fire or building code inspectors.

When a water main must be repaired or extended, citizens should be told when and for how long the water will be cut off.

Announcements in newspapers and on the radio should warn motorists about streets that will be closed for repairs. In addition, prominent signs should be posted on and near the streets that will be closed.

If a branch library must be closed for renovation, post notices in all libraries and use newspaper and radio announcements.

Know your government

Your local government is the sum of many parts: paid employees, local taxes, streets and parks, libraries and other buildings, trucks and police cars, and state laws and local ordinances that make it possible for you and others to get your work done. The "identity" of the local government will come from

the way its people think and feel about it. The neighborhood trash collector, the police officer directing traffic in the rain, the inspector of weights and measures in a grocery store or supermarket, the ticket collector at the zoo, the secretary behind the desk, the technician in the public health laboratory, the supervisor at a playground all give the government they represent an identity.

To help make sure your government has a positive identity, you as a supervisor should have some knowledge and understanding of your government's services, taxes, and officials. Remember that most citizens do not go to the mayor, the city or county manager, or a government department head to have their questions answered. If you live on the street, they probably will ask you why the water rate went up or when the recreation department's baseball league starts. If you (or your employees) can give a complete and accurate answer, you will have done your part for public relations.

Do you and your employees know enough about your government? Ask yourself these questions:

How much do I know about departments and divisions other than my own?

How many officials do I know by name?

When was the last time I attended a council or board meeting? (Was that the

It is good public relations to let people know in advance when public improvements and repairs are scheduled.

time salaries for my department were being reviewed?)

Do I read the bulletins and announcements distributed to supervisors and employees?

Do I discuss bulletins, announcements, and other kinds of information with employees in my work group?

You and your workers can keep informed about your government by reading the employee newsletter, bulletin board notices, memos, the annual report, and whatever other sources of information your government publishes.

Services

In a general way you should know what programs and services are provided by your city or county government. Nobody expects you to be an expert in immunology, library classification, or cost accounting, but you should know generally what your city or county does and where to go for further information. If your local government issues an annual report, this is an excellent place to get an overview of the services your local government provides.

Taxes

In these days of tax and expenditure limitations, almost everybody is concerned about who pays for what. It is a good idea to learn something about your city or county taxes, especially the property tax. In many parts of the country, the taxes for public schools make up one-half to two-thirds of the total property tax bill—a fact that many people don't know. The annual report for your local government and various tax leaflets and fliers will provide most of the information you need. When you don't have the answer, you can refer people to the finance department.

City council or county board

Be sure you know the names of the members of the city council or county board or at least, in a larger city or county, the name of the council or board member from your ward or district. People may ask you questions on primary and general elections, the composition of the city council or county board, and the kinds of powers they have. In most parts of the country the city council or the county board can adopt local ordinances and local taxes but not state laws or state taxes. This may seem obvious to you, but many people are not aware that state and local governments have different zones of authority.

Know yourself

You probably find that you can communicate better with your spouse, your children, close friends, and a few people at work than you can with people you know only casually. One of the reasons is that you know your family and friends well and you trust them. You have a lot in common with them, and you have, therefore, developed interpersonal communication that works well for both senders and receivers.

You can use interpersonal communication to develop better working relations with employees and others whom you do not know as well. It is important to remember that everything about you communicates. Your ability as a supervisor often is measured by what and how well you communicate. Let's look again at some of the elements of communication mentioned in Chapter 5.

Personal appearance

Appearances do matter. How a person looks is important to other people. The public will judge the attitude and abilities of local government employees by the way they look. An office full of people with messy hair, dirty fingernails, and rumpled clothing conveys a message of indifference or dislike. Dirty uniforms on a work crew say that these employees do not care—either about themselves or about others.

Surroundings are important, too. Furniture, machines, and equipment should be well lighted, clean, and well maintained. An automotive repair garage can be just as neat and well organized as an office. Street construction and repair work should include good lighting, signs, and barricades to convey a message of concern for the safety and convenience of the public.

The way you talk

Whether you talk with a regional accent or with the neutrality of radio and television announcers, the way your words are expressed as well as their content carries a message. Sometimes it is helpful to speak slowly and distinctly to give a citizen or a co-worker time to absorb information. Often the person you are talking to (the receiver) must tune in before he or she can begin to follow what you are saying.

The same care is needed when you are listening. If you do not pay attention, the person will be talking at you and you will not understand completely the message coming to you. Sometimes this works both ways. When you are talking the other person doesn't listen, and when the other person is talking you are not listening. If you are not sure you understand, it helps to repeat information to make sure that you and the other person are talking about the same thing.

Personal behavior

Your surroundings, your appearance, and the way you talk come together in your personal behavior, which either helps or hinders in getting messages across. Here are some suggestions that may be helpful:

Stay away from words that put your audience on the defensive. Evaluative and judgmental words, such as "stupid," "incompetent," and "crummy," are high-risk words. They are likely to irritate and anger people. When someone is talking, do not interrupt to finish his or her message. Give that person a chance to say what he or she is saying. Watch the use of jokes and humor that may offend, especially jokes that are sexist, racist, or off-color.

Take your time. Listen carefully. When you are asked a question, phrase your reply to make it as clear as possible.

Be careful that you do not overagree or nod too much while the other person is talking. You may think your behavior conveys understanding, but the sender of the message may think that you are not listening.

Don't fidget, doodle, look out the window, or otherwise fail to concentrate when someone is talking to you. If you do not have time to talk, say so, but then be sure to give the person a chance to talk to you later.

Questions and complaints

Answering questions and dealing with complaints from homeowners, business operators, public officials, and other citizens is part of a day's work. Questions and complaints usually come in three forms: in person, on the phone, or through the mail. All require prompt, courteous, and accurate replies.

Complaints are especially important because they are danger signals that something is wrong. If complaints are given prompt, careful attention, your city or county can improve its services as well as its public relations.

Your employees should know that complaints must be investigated and corrected promptly. Once the source of the problem has been found, the citizen should be told what will (or will not) be done and why. It is important to find out also whether the problem has been corrected and to ask the person who complained if there is anything else you and other employees can do to help straighten matters out.

Questions and complaints should be considered together because a question that is poorly handled will often lead to a complaint.

Face to face

The best way to handle either a question or a complaint is face to face, especially if the problem is technical. It is easier because both you and the citizen can observe each other, listen to each other, ask questions to clarify other questions, and agree on the facts.

It is important not only to be pleasant and polite but also to be convincing. Could you look a citizen straight in the eye and say: "My name is Jessica Jones. I work for your city government, and I am here for the sole purpose of serving you." Perhaps you would be embarrassed at this grand language, but you should not be embarrassed to put it this way: "My name is Jessica Jones, and it's my job as an employee of this city to help you work this out."

Take a look at these specific suggestions and see how many you can apply.

When someone approaches you, always acknowledge that person's presence either by speaking or by nodding if you are engaged in some other important task and cannot talk to the person immediately. Remember, nobody likes to be ignored.

Do not blame the person who brings a question. Instead, look at the question as a chance to provide information and possibly to correct some aspect of the program in your local government that is deficient.

Pay attention and show interest. Sometimes a helpful way to do this is to ask questions yourself to be sure that both you and the citizen are talking about the same thing.

Provide as much information as you can, factually and promptly. Do not make excuses.

Do not argue. Do not try to blame your department, your city or county government, or anyone else.

Whether it is a question or a complaint, help the person to find the information if you don't have it. If necessary, refer the person to the right office or agency either in your government or elsewhere. If you do not know where to send the person for further information, help him or her by looking it up.

Give the person the benefit of the doubt. If your city or county is wrong, say so. Admission that your local government can be wrong helps to humanize that government in the eyes of the citizens who are served.

Telephone

The telephone is a popular way to handle questions and complaints. It is quick, easy, and inexpensive. Think about how you may sound on the phone. You may think your phone voice is businesslike and efficient, but the person on the other end of the line may think it is brusque or cold. To make the best use of the telephone, the following guidelines should be observed.

Answer the phone promptly.

Identify yourself and your department.

Speak clearly, naturally, and distinctly.

Keep a pencil and paper next to the phone to note important information and messages.

If the caller is upset, remain calm, listen carefully, and do not argue. Get the facts.

If a call must be transferred, relay all pertinent information to the person to whom the call is transferred, so that the caller does not have to repeat the question or complaint from the beginning.

Do not keep the caller waiting while you are looking up information. If necessary, tell the person that you need time to look up the information and that you will call back as soon as possible.

Be careful with the "hold" button! If you put someone on hold, make it short—twenty to thirty seconds at the most.

Deliver all phone messages promptly to prevent delays in returning calls or embarrassment to the person for whom the call was intended.

End a telephone call as courteously as it began; a good final impression is important.

Letters and memoranda

Writing is difficult for most people. And in many governments, it is overdone. Therefore, before you begin to write a letter, ask yourself whether a phone call or a face-to-face conversation would get the job done better and easier. If you decide that a letter is necessary, give some thought to its form and content. You might ask yourself what the purpose of the letter is. What do you expect the letter to achieve? Making a simple outline first can help you write a good letter. Make clear in your conclusion what you expect the receiver of the letter to do. Just as in speaking, the language in the letter should be simple, clear, and direct. After you have drafted the letter, you may want to read it again to see whether a call or a face-to-face conversation might be better after all.

In some government offices, memoranda are used to excess. Therefore, before you write a memorandum, ask yourself: "Is this memo necessary?" Often a phone call is better. Look for shortcuts. If you get a lengthy memorandum about a staff meeting, it may be enough to put your name in the upper right-hand corner, write "I will be there," and return the memo to the sender.

How to say no

No matter how polite you are, no matter how carefully you speak and listen, no matter how

Two ways to say no.

conscientiously you put information together, the time inevitably comes when you have to say "no." Most of us would rather say yes, but this is not always possible. It is, therefore, important to learn to say no in a way that people understand and accept.

Suppose, for example, a resident wants permission to build within five yards of the property line and you know the minimum zoning setback is ten yards. You could say, "No, you can't do it." But a better way of saying no might be: "Five yards from your property line? Let's take a look at the code, Mrs. Humphrey, and see if we can find a way for you to do that."

At this point, you and Mrs. Humphrey look at the housing and zoning code regulations together. "Here it is. Oh my, it says, 'side yard setback must be ten yards.' I am afraid it cannot be done in this case. I am sorry, but the code will not allow you to build within five yards of your property line."

Going through this procedure helps the citizen understand why the request cannot be granted. Besides, she realizes you have done all you can. It is not you or the "government" but the code that is preventing her from doing what she wants to do.

When you have to say no, you should break the news as gently and courteously as possible. At the same time you must make it